DRAGONS'
DEN

GROW YOUR
BUSINESS

HOW TO EXPAND
FROM SMALL TO BIG

MICHAEL HEATH, PETER SPALTON, STUART WARNER

Collins

A division of HarperCollins*Publishers*
77-85 Fulham Palace Road, London W6 8JB
First published in Great Britain in 2010 by HarperCollins*Publishers*
1
Copyright © HarperCollins*Publishers* 2010
Michael Heath, Peter Spalton and Stuart Warner assert the moral right
to be identified as the authors of this work.

Foreword copyright © Evan Davis 2010

A catalogue record for this book is available from the British Library.
ISBN 978-0-00-736426-8

Dragons' Den

Created by Nippon Television Network Corporation
This book is produced under licence from 2waytraffic, a Sony Pictures Entertainment
company/CPT Holdings. Dragons' Den and all associated logos, images and trade marks
are owned and controlled by 2waytraffic.

Produced by Thameside Media
www.thamesidemedia.com

Printed and bound by Graficas Estella, Spain

Mixed Sources
Product group from well-managed
forests and other controlled sources
www.fsc.org Cert no. SW-COC-001806
© 1996 Forest Stewardship Council
FSC

FSC is a non-profit international organisation established to promote the
responsible management of the world's forests. Products carrying the FSC
label are independently certified to assure consumers that they come
from forests that are managed to meet the social, economic and
ecological needs of present and future generations.

Find out more about HarperCollins and the environment at
www.harpercollins.co.uk/green

ABOUT THE AUTHORS

Michael Heath is Managing Director of Michael Heath Consulting, a Learning and Development Consultancy established in 1999. Having worked with an impressive portfolio of international organizations, he offers a wealth of practical knowledge about the management of growing businesses. He is the author of *Management* and *Leadership* in the Business Secrets series, also published by HarperCollins.

Peter Spalton is a professional Speaker and Business Consultant whose clients include multinationals, public bodies and private companies. He is a member of the Professional Speakers' Association and has held senior marketing positions in ICL, Ericsson and Nokia. He is the author of *Dragons' Den: The Perfect Pitch* and also *Marketing* in HarperCollins's Business Secrets series.

Stuart Warner is a Chartered Accountant and Director of Financial Fluency Ltd. He trains people for recognized professional qualifications and offers related development training to management and staff at all levels. He currently advises the board of one of the UK's top Accounting Institutes and is the author of *Finance Basics* in HarperCollins's Business Secrets series.

CONTENTS

FOREWORD

FROM DRAGONS' DEN HOST
EVAN DAVIS

When you ask young children what they want to be when they grow up, they venture a range of answers from ballet dancers to astronauts (and now, in no short measure thanks to Dragons' Den, successful entrepreneurs).

It's great for children to dream about adulthood in this way. But when they get older and are ready to leave school, few people would advise them to cling to their infant fantasies. There's no point in a young boy dreaming of a successful life as a ballet dancer if he lacks the physique to achieve that. A good career is not just one that would be nice to have; it is one that is attainable. One might go so far as to say that the definition of growing up is when children learn to contain their imagination and realize instead that they need to focus on practical outcomes. Well, what is true for children is true for entrepreneurs too.

It's important for you to dream: to be ambitious for your company and to think about what you would like it to be when it grows big. But there is also a time when you have to let the practicalities of life intrude into the dreams. It is the achievable that matters as much as the desirable. Many successful entrepreneurs come unstuck when they fail to realize this, and grow too far or in the wrong direction.

What does this imply? Before you embark on a major growth path, you need to question your own objectives and subject them to rigorous criticism. Perhaps the best way of going about this is to be as tough on yourself as a Dragon would be. Think to yourself, "what would a Dragon ask me about my plans? Would they be convinced by them?" There is surely no better way of testing your strategy.

This book will help you with that. It provides a checklist of the sorts of issues that the Dragons might raise if you were standing in front of them pitching your growth plan. The chapters are built around 10 important Commandments that govern the whys, the wheres, the hows and of course the 'how much' of growth. It will help you avoid the pitfalls and it will help discipline your thinking about the many possibilities. I do hope you read it thoroughly before you let your company grow too big.

Evan Davis

COMMANDMENT 1

EXPAND YOUR HORIZONS

Is it the right time to grow?

CONGRATULATIONS! You're now the owner of a business that is going places. You're turning over a decent profit and suddenly all that hard work is reaping rewards. But you've come to a crossroads and every road that leads off into the future seems to have its own roadblocks. So what do you do? Stay as you are or expand? This chapter gets you thinking about the right things: is now the right time? What are the pros and cons of expanding your business? And what will the effect be on your time and health? Then there's the whole premises issue. That new building might be roomy, glitzy and swish, and looking like a good deal on a 10-year lease, but what if you outgrow it in three years?

WHY GROW THE BUSINESS?

Do you really need to expand? This may be a simple enough question but it's going to demand some serious and thoughtful consideration on your part. Here are a couple of facts for you: in the UK 25% of businesses go belly up in the first year. By the fifth year that figure is round about 80%. So the good news is you've probably cleared the first statistic! But how can you make sure that you don't make decisions now that mean your business ends up in the corporate graveyard with the other 80%?

Usually businesses expand because they see opportunities that they want to take advantage of. The reasons you might be considering expanding could be:

1 You would like to sell more of your product or service to your existing customers.

WHEN D4M'S JULIA CHARLES *went into the Den (see pp28–9), her company was having to turn down work. The business had grown organically, based on word of mouth, and now they were running at capacity with their current set-up and the personel simply couldn't take on more work. Feeling that it was a bad idea to be turning down business, Julia wanted investment to do two things: to take on more staff in order to, effectively, sell more of their services to the customers who were already coming to them; and to have a dedicated marketing employee to broaden their client base.*

**BABY BATH TOWEL
COMPANY CUDDLEDRY**
*(see pp202–3) expanded
the age range of their
products in reaction to
consumer feedback. As their
babies were growing up,
customers wanted similarly
fun bath and beach towels
for their growing toddlers.
So Cuddledry came up
with a range of towels and
bathrobes for toddlers
and older children as an
additional line to their
core range.*

**AND CUDDLEDRY MOVED
INTO THE PET MARKET TOO,**
*with a towel aimed at
pampered pooches. This was
a suggestion from one of the
Dragons, James Caan.*

2   You have spotted a new market which you know your
     current products or services meet.

3   You would like to offer new products or services to the
     customers you already have.

4   You would like to offer new products or services to new
     customers or a new market.

Where many entrepreneurs go wrong is by believing that by getting bigger, they will automatically generate more profits. This often isn't the case. You'll need to think about how the costs that go with expansion are more than offset by the growth in profits.

Later on in this chapter we'll be looking at how expansion is going to eat into your time and, if you're not careful, eat into your health. Have you discussed the expansion with those closest to you: your friends and family? Are they ready for the demands that you will place on them? If your business grows, will you be in a position to meet your responsibilities to the people you care about?

" I REALLY LIKE TO SEE PEOPLE START FROM QUITE SMALL, AND GROW " DEBORAH MEADEN, DRAGON

THE PROS AND CONS OF EXPANDING YOUR BUSINESS

Growth is an essential part of any business. But you need to make sure that you don't allow the growth of your business to balloon at a faster rate than you are able to control.

This is the time to apply some sound business thinking to your dilemma. So here are some important questions that you must be able to answer with a convincing "Yes" if you are going to grow successfully.

IN SERIES 6, THEO PAPHITIS GAVE LESLEY-ANN SIMMONS OF SHOES GALORE *some sound advice about expanding too quickly. Lesley-Ann had a franchise shoe-selling business. It worked on what's known as a 'party plan', whereby franchisees organize social gatherings at which to sell the shoes. Lesley-Ann had wanted to expand her base of franchisees, until Theo warned her about the danger of tying up too much cash in providing stock for the franchisees. It can work in the long run, but in the short term Lesley-Ann could suddenly face cash flow problems – the killer of many a small business (see also pp100–1).*

- **HAVE YOU THE RIGHT PEOPLE IN PLACE?** Have the people in your business really got the talent, commitment and ability to help you grow?

- **HAVE YOU THE RIGHT OPPORTUNITIES?** Are there definitely potential needs and gaps that exist in the marketplace that your business could successfully meet?

PROWASTE MANAGEMENT DIRECTOR PAUL TINTON *appeared in the Den in Series 6 (see p219). Timing was crucial to his pitch. He explained to the Dragons that in 2008 a law had come into force compelling construction companies to do more about recycling waste materials by preparing a Site Waste Management Programme (SWMP) before beginning work on projects with a cost of more than £300,000. Paul realized that a business that could provide a 'one-stop shop' for sorting this out – preparing the SWMP then enacting it by collecting and recycling the site waste – would be on to a winner. Having gained investment from Deborah and Duncan, Paul relocated the business closer to his client base in London and is successfully providing the recycling requirements at development sites for clients such as Arup and Parkeray.*

- **ARE YOU CONVINCED ABOUT THE TIMING?** Is now really the best time to expand? What are the economic, regulatory or competitive factors that have convinced you this is the right time?

- **WILL YOU GET THE RIGHT RETURN FOR THE RISK YOU'RE GOING TO TAKE?** Is the potential profit really worth the investment in money and time you're about to commit?

" DON'T EVER TAKE YOUR EYE OFF THE BALL AS TO WHY YOU ARE IN BUSINESS: PROFIT. TURNOVER CAN BLIND YOU. "

LORD SUGAR, BUSINESS MOGUL

It's time to draw up a list. First, look at the reasons that support the expansion. You can use the checklist here. Then, look at the disadvantages of expansion.

ADVANTAGES OF EXPANSION

- **GREATER PROFITS.** This is the reason why most directors want to expand their business. But as we asked before: are you sure more business means more profits?

- **ECONOMIES OF SCALE.** Perhaps you want to open up another retail outlet? Move into an adjacent market? Whatever it is, you probably are going to have common functions that can support both.

- **RAISING THE PROFILE OF THE COMPANY.** Being bigger may well give you greater presence in your marketplace. It's certainly going to send positive messages to your existing client base.

- **OFFERING A GREATER RANGE TO YOUR CUSTOMERS.** Growth may well mean that you can be more comprehensive with what you offer, supplementing your products and services with new initiatives.

- **RAISING THE CONFIDENCE AND STATUS OF YOUR EMPLOYEES.** It's great to work for a successful organization, especially when you were there at the beginning!

DISADVANTAGES OF EXPANSION

- **GREATER DEMANDS ON YOUR TIME.** How well are you coping with the time management issues at the moment? Have you enough hours in the day to get the expansion working? See Managing Your Health after this list.

- **LOSING FOCUS.** Small companies are usually finely tuned to their respective markets. Will growth mean doing many things adequately rather than one thing brilliantly? We look at the marketplace in detail in Commandments 2, 3 and 4.

- **CASH FLOW ISSUES.** This is the real killer for many expanding businesses. Are you sure you have enough cash entering the business to support the greater demands that expansion inevitably brings? We look at cash flow and other money issues in Commandment 5.

- **GOING TO OTHERS FOR FINANCE.** Perhaps, up to now, you've financed the business yourself. Are you prepared to go out and find new investors to generate the money you need to bankroll the expansion? Finance-sourcing is covered in Commandment 6.

- **BRINGING IN NEW EMPLOYEES.** You can't do everything, but will the new people you get in do it the way you want, to the standard you want? Commandment 7 helps you recruit the right people.

- **LOSING CONTROL.** You can't be everywhere at once. Will you be able to delegate without hovering over people to see it's done properly? Leadership skills are covered in Commandment 8.

- **GREATER COMPLEXITY.** If you always prided yourself on keeping things simple, you're going to find it a real challenge getting the new processes and procedures under control. Commandment 9 will help you set up efficient systems for an expanding business.

MANAGING YOUR HEALTH

A dead entrepreneur is no good to anybody. The stress that goes with running a business isn't always obvious. Stress often slips into your presence without you seeing it and, before you've realized it was even there, has already done its worst. So you must look after yourself. Tiredness causes business accidents that can't always be repaired.

Some people take long working hours in their stride, but the price most of us pay is a gradual decline in our health and well-being. Where's the sense of building a great business if you don't live long enough to see it flourish?

GET THE WORK-LIFE BALANCE RIGHT

Owning your own business has a habit of sucking in all of your energy and time. It can become a black hole of need, making endless demands on your attention and, like a jealous lover, pulling you away from everything else that once mattered in your life.

So you must be kind to yourself. Make some firm rules that create space for the other things that are important to you. Your partner. Your family. Your interests. Your sleep. Yourself.

THINK ABOUT THE BUSINESS PURPOSE – AND YOUR PURPOSE IN IT

People like to put other people into boxes. They might ask, "Do you live to work – or work to live?" For many entrepreneurs, the purpose of their business becomes the purpose of their whole existence. The trouble is, the business starts to define them: if the business is a success, they are a success. If the business fails – then, surely, they must be a failure.

But this is too simplistic. Far better the business owner who looks first for what they want from life – the motivation that gives meaning to who they are and what they do. For one person it might be to live life on the edge. For another it could be the desire to provide security for themselves or their loved ones. What's yours? It's an important question to ask, and one that will be a far better measure of whether you're a success or not.

LAURA AND NEIL WESTWOOD'S MAGIC WHITEBOARD BUSINESS *had been growing rapidly when they made their pitch in Series 6. They had been operating from their home until then, but, after having secured investment from Deborah and Theo, it was time to take the business to the next level and move to more appropriate premises. The business was doing extremely well, but, rather than put money into plush town-centre offices, the couple focused on the kind of location that would continue to drive the business forward. They are now renting basic, inexpensive offices right next to a haulage firm that they use for distribution – not pretty, but very functional.*

The business purpose has its own life. You can call it a mission statement if you want. But there must be some overarching purpose that your business will work towards.

Your role is to use this purpose as a yardstick against which you can assess all of your activities. Better still, as you grow and new people come on board, you can make sure that their efforts, decisions and behaviour all correspond to – and serve – this purpose.

LABAN ROOMES'S GOLDGENIE BUSINESS *(see p155) made a more upmarket move than Magic Whiteboard's, but essentially it was for similar reasons: location. In Laban's case, the move was to be right in the centre of London's jewellery trade in Hatton Garden.*

WHERE WILL YOUR LARGER BUSINESS LIVE?

It is well known that, for many business owners, the second highest outgoing they have after wages is property costs. Perhaps you're considering new, bigger, premises to work in? Maybe you're already fed up with tripping over valuable stock, document boxes and employees! When considering new premises you must keep your ego firmly in check. New premises can be an exciting option, but you must give serious thought to the decision before you start looking. Here are just some factors that might help your decision:

- **COSTS** Will the new premises be significantly more expensive? Can you justify the business need? Will increased profits adequately absorb the additional cost?

- **RENT OR BUY?** Will renting be kinder to your cash flow? If you buy, are you prepared for the hassle that owning property always brings? The blocked toilets, the leaking roof...

- **REGULATIONS** What regulations govern the property? Does the building have the necessary permissions to allow you to conduct your business (e.g. noise levels, machinery safety, etc.)?

- **GROWTH** How quickly are you likely to outgrow the new premises? Will the terms of your lease constrain you when you need to expand further? Conversely, will you be locking yourself into a lease for costly premises that may prove to be too large for your organization's needs?

- **EMPLOYEES** How accessible will the new premises be for them? Will their travel costs increase?

- **CUSTOMERS** Is passing trade important? Does the location get you close to the customers that matter?

- **LOCATION** Do you need easy access to motorways or other transport links? Will a new location increase costs for you? Will staff have access to local amenities?

- **SUPPLIERS** Can they get to you quickly? Will there be an increase in delivery costs?

" THE WHOLE WORLD WANTS TO BE SUCCESSFUL. WHAT I TRY TO DO IS SEPARATE 'WANT' FROM 'NEED'. NEED IS HUNGER, DRIVE, DETERMINATION AND TENACITY. PEOPLE WHO MERELY 'WANT' DON'T HAVE THAT. " JAMES CAAN, DRAGON

- **COMPETITORS** Are you placing yourself at greater risk by going head-to-head with a much stronger competitor in the area? Conversely, will it place you in an area with a reputation for the products and services your business sells (e.g. estate agents, accountants, etc.)?

HEALTH AND SAFETY

If you have never employed people at your premises before, you will need to make sure you meet the minimum health and safety standards. If you already employ people, but need to take on more, remember these key areas that may need upgrading in terms of health and safety:

- Making sure toilets are sanitary.
- Complying with fire safety standards.
- Maintaining standards which are industry specific (e.g. use of protective clothing, etc.).
- Ensuring that machinery and other equipment is used safely by your employees.

- Having a proper accident reporting procedure in place.
- Conducting proper risk assessments.

INSURANCE

You will probably have to upgrade your insurance for larger premises, or take on forms of insurance that you didn't need before. Different policies can include:

- Public & Employers' Liability (Employers' Liability Insurance is a statutory obligation).
- Cover for Business Interruption.
- Business Contents Insurance.
- Buildings Insurance.
- Any other insurance specific to your business activity.

WHO CAN HELP?

In the first instance a chartered surveyor is the expert to consult about your premises. They can assess the structural state of the building and whether alterations will be needed to make the building fit for your business purpose. The Health and Safety Executive's website (www.hse.gov.uk) gives detailed information and advice. If you need information about making the building accessible then you should contact the Equality and Human Rights Commission (www.equalityhumanrights.com).

Your solicitor should analyse the terms and conditions of any agreement in case there are any unfair terms that you might be unaware of. Your Local Authority or relevant trade body may also be able to provide further advice.

D4M

Julia Charles founded events business D4M in 2002. It was running with a turnover of £225,000, a staff of four and a net profit of £24,000 at the time of Julia's pitch to the Dragons in 2008. There had been growing demand for D4M's services, and Julia wanted to take on a full-time person to handle marketing and clients so that she could expand the set-up to take on more work.

JULIA *venturing into the Den in 2008.*

Dragon Deborah Meaden, with experience of the sector, thought that there wasn't enough profit potential to attract outside investment to the company, but two pairings, Theo and Peter, and Duncan and James, both made equal offers: all the money for a 40% stake. They put up good cases for demanding such a high stake, and Julia, awed by the amount of interest, accepted this and focused instead on which pairing of Dragons suited D4M best.

James stressed that he was interested in investing in D4M as a team of young, entrepreneurial individuals, financing and facilitating their dynamism and vision. It was James and Duncan's offer that Julia accepted in the Den.

The nature of the deal struck subsequently changed, however. Firstly, James took over Duncan's portion of the investment, meaning that he alone had the 40% investment stake. But then the ripples of the recession hit the corporate entertainment industry. Mutually they decided that with the reduction in revenue, Julia needed to keep the profits herself rather than see 40% disappearing. This was more crucial than investment in a period of recession, so Julia paid back the money that James had invested.

Since regaining 100% control of her business, Julia

JULIA TOOK ALONG ONE OF D4M'S QUIRKY TOUCHES *for corporate events: a person disguised as an ornamental plant to surprise guests.*

has been much happier anyway. "I knew what was involved in giving away part of the business, but then the realization kicked in that obviously I had to, not exactly work underneath somebody, but it just felt like I wasn't in control any more."

JULIA HAS SAID, *"What I was dreaming for, I got, and actually it wasn't what I wanted. Now I'm me again. I've got my passion back."*

COMMANDMENT 2

DISCOVER OPPORTUNITIES FOR GROWTH

How can your business expand?

IF YOU THINK ABOUT IT, there are three major ways you can grow your business: you can introduce a new product or service, conquer a new market or acquire other companies. Theoretically it's possible to do all three at once, but we're not going to suggest that you rush to do so – that could lead to disaster! Rather, this chapter shows you how to assess your business for potential growth, bearing in mind important factors such as the marketplace and the competition. A closer look at finding new markets follows in Commandment 3, and Commandment 4 delves further into the ways you can exploit different outlets.

In order to work out which approach to growth you should take, you must decide what sort of company you are. Most small and new companies tend to work at the leading edge of technology, whereas bigger companies are often followers at the other end of the spectrum. For example, Apple might appear to be leading edge, but it is actually usually second or third into the market in terms of new technology. What it is good at is repackaging existing technology to create original and aesthetic product designs.

All products and technologies have a life; they go from conception through maturity and into death and decline. Sometimes the lifespan is only a matter of months, as in the case of some toy crazes, but usually the lifespan is years. For example, the cathode ray tube, which was first introduced in the 1920s and used in televisions for decades, is now in decline since the emergence of plasma, LCD and other screen technologies that are lighter and less bulky. In marketing terminology this lifespan phenomenon is called the **PRODUCT LIFE CYCLE (PLC)**. Most companies prefer to operate in just one part of the PLC as it suits their culture and management style.

- **CONCEPTION AND DEVELOPMENT STAGE.** Companies working at the beginning of the Product Life Cycle conceive and develop new technologies. They then license these to other companies to manufacture, market and sell. University departments, start-ups from academia and spin-offs from government research agencies are good examples of this type of organization. Others include companies like Cosworth who licensed its foundry technology to Ford in the 1970s.

PRODUCTS SUCH AS THE WHEELIE BIN LID LIFTER (RIGHT) AND THE GRILLSTREAM *(both of which appeared in Series 7) can, in retrospect at least, be seen as entrepreneurs working at the conception and development stage of the product life cycle. In both cases, the entrepreneurs had working prototypes that they demonstrated in the Den, and in both cases they have since used the licensing route as a way to make income from the ideas without having to be involved in the manufacture, marketing and sales of the products. The financial rewards tend to be less, but so is the level of risk and investment of time and work. It can free those who are best at innovation to concentrate on that area with further projects.*

- **LAUNCH AND INTRODUCTION STAGE.** Some companies prefer to take existing or new technologies and turn them into products. These are the companies that work at the leading edge, designing, developing and introducing products into the market. They're not usually into mass production and don't have the sales capacity to exploit the whole market. But they're quite happy to sell their products to people who like new products. This type of customer is known as an **EARLY ADOPTER** – they love to buy leading-edge and innovative products. Some of the mobile phone companies, such as Palm and Sony-

PRODUCTS SUCH AS SHEWEE (SERIES 2, ABOVE) AND MAGNAMOLE (SERIES 7, LEFT) *were pitched in the Den by entrepreneurs who were determined to launch and introduce their inventions to market. In both cases the inventors, Samantha Fountain and Sharon Wright respectively, had addressed a problem and come up with a solution that they'd developed into a saleable product. Samantha's invention, the Shewee, enables women to urinate while standing up. For the past few years, Samantha has been pursuing her ambition and is trading in domestic and overseas markets, selling the Shewee into the sports and health sectors. Sharon Wright's invention, Magnamole, is a magnetic device for speedily threading cables through cavity walls. Sharon is in the early stages of taking her product to markets worldwide.*

Ericsson, are examples of leading-edge companies. The UK's Modec is another. It manufactures and sells limited numbers of electric delivery vehicles.

- **GROWTH AND MATURITY STAGE.** This covers the companies that operate in the mass market. They are often known as **FOLLOWERS** and have the resources to manufacture, market and sell products in large quantities. They are not interested in small volumes and they have the classic "stack 'em high and sell 'em cheap" philosophy. Many of the large companies who operate in **FMCG MARKETS** (fast-moving consumer goods) adopt this approach. They have marketing muscle and obtain new technologies and products from the smaller companies that operate at the leading edge.

If you are a small and innovative company you will probably be happiest in the launch and introduction stage of the Product Life Cycle. Typically you wouldn't go for volume, so you must always have new products coming down the track in your development pipeline. The key issue is that the management style and culture are very different between leading-edge and mass-marketing companies.

It is very rare for organizations to work across all stages of the product life cycle. Exceptions are companies like 3M and Audi who have successfully created a business structure that works at all these different levels. At the other end of the scale, Mercedes, Renault, BMW and Toyota are mass producers who have used their Formula 1 racing teams to develop new technologies which they feed into their products many years later.

" IF OPPORTUNITY DOESN'T KNOCK, BUILD A DOOR "

MILTON BERLE, AMERICAN TV STAR

SERVICING STOP *(see p36) is a good example of a business seeking to grow through taking more market share. In a relatively short period of time, they had developed a decent level of business. But that was only a small fraction of the potential market and, to get more of it, they needed to push brand awareness to increase their market share.*

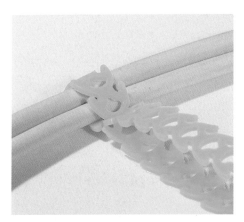

SIMILARLY RAPSTRAP *wanted to take more of the cable tie market. In its case, though, it wasn't brand awareness that was the principal obstacle, it was simply not being able to manufacture sufficient quantities to supply demand. Dragon investment made that possible and Rapstrap is now successfully penetrating the market in the UK and abroad.*

YOUR CHOICES FOR GROWTH

Business is often compared to a war where companies battle it out for a share of the customer's money. Assuming you are the owner of a small business, your pockets probably won't be deep enough to fight the big guns head on. You will therefore have to fight a 'guerrilla campaign'. This type of war will play to your strengths as a small business – you can be flexible, fast moving and innovative.

You have four choices, which in classic marketing are known as the **ANSOFF MATRIX.** (This is named after Igor Ansoff who first published the concept in the September 1957 issue of the *Harvard Business Review*.)

- **SELL MORE OF THE SAME.**
You can sell more of your current products into your existing market. In other words, go for market share.

- **SELL CURRENT PRODUCTS TO NEW MARKETS.** You can find and exploit new markets for your existing products. Marketing people call this market development and we will cover this in Chapter Three.

- **SELL NEW PRODUCTS TO CURRENT MARKETS.** You can find or develop some new products that you can sell into your existing markets. We call this product development.

PHYSICOOL'S KAY RUSSELL *had an existing equine business when she made an appearance in the Den in Series 7. She had always been involved in the breeding and training of horses, and had developed a reusable cooling bandage and spray for use on muscle injuries. Realizing that the same product could be equally effective for people with sports injuries, Kay decided to set up a separate company retailing the same, but differently branded, product for the sports sector. Recognizing the need for separate identities for the businesses geared towards the human and equine markets, Deborah Meaden offered £100,000 for a 30% stake in Physicool.*

- **SELL SOMETHING COMPLETELY DIFFERENT.** This is diversification, and one major way to achieve it is to buy another business and merge it with your own. We talk more about acquisition in Commandment 10.

Just because there are four ways to grow, you don't have to rigidly stick to a single approach. Often it's best if you can mix and match Ansoff's choices to suit your own market situation.

HOW TO DO MORE OF THE SAME

In Ansoff's terminology, this is selling more of your existing products into your existing markets. If your product has 'repeatability', then you should encourage your customers to consume more. Price promotions can help you do this as they encourage people to spend more of their disposable income on your products. The alternative is to convince them that using more of your product is good for them – this is relatively easy with health and personal care products, and harder with things like alcohol or domestic appliances.

If your product isn't one that people will buy again and again, you will have to devise a way to penetrate the market. There are two possible strategies that you can adopt to take a bigger share of the market:

- **TARGET NON-USERS.** Sell to people who don't buy either your product or a competitor's.

- **TARGET YOUR COMPETITORS' USERS.** Convince your competitors' customers to switch to your product instead.

SERVICING STOP

Toby and Oliver Richmond's business, Servicing Stop, is an agency for servicing vehicles using a wide network of independent garages in the UK. It competes with the manufacturers' own dealerships on price primarily, but also on service, by collecting and dropping off vehicles to and from home or work addresses and having the cars cleaned after each service.

THE BROTHERS MADE A SOLID PITCH *in which they outlined the potential of a market in which customers were increasingly looking for better value than that offered by authorized car dealerships.*

Though the business had been running for only a year when the brothers ventured into the Den in 2009, it was clearly a successful business model. Their year one turnover was £1.5 million, with a net profit of £120,000. The business was expanding rapidly and they wanted to establish it quickly as a nationwide business. Indeed, the amount they were spending on advertising and marketing (£30,000 per month) showed the brothers' commitment to their vision of expansion.

Three Dragons offered the £100,000 they were seeking to push on the marketing front, and the brothers accepted Deborah's deal for a 30% stake in the business.

SELLING TO NON-USERS

People aren't using either your product or any of your competitors' for reasons such as they don't need it, they think it's too expensive, they've never heard about it or they can't get it. If it's the last two reasons, you need to spend money on marketing or find other ways to sell your product. (We cover the latter in Commandment 4.)

" IF YOU ATTACK YOUR MARKET FROM MULTIPLE POSITIONS AND YOUR COMPETITION DOESN'T, YOU HAVE ALL THE ADVANTAGE "

JAY ABRAHAM, MARKETING GURU

If people aren't buying because they think it's too expensive or don't need it, you could develop a completely new product or create a number of slightly different variations. To do this you should think about what you could remove to create a cheaper version, or what you could add to create a more expensive product.

We often talk about markets with ends. There are products at the bottom end, ones in the mid range and others at the top end. Car manufacturers create a series of models that cover the whole spectrum: they have a basic version, a mid-range version and a sporty model. If you look at a typical piece of software that you'd buy off the internet, you will probably find that it's available in three or four different versions, as shown opposite.

TYPICAL SOFTWARE VERSIONS

- A **FREE COPY** which has limited features and may include on-screen advertising. For a small charge you can easily upgrade to the next version, unlock some more features and remove the advertising.

- The **'LITE' PRODUCT** has more features and no advertising. It is aimed at the home-user who can upgrade to the professional product for another small charge.

- The **PROFESSIONAL VERSION** has all the features, but in a stand alone format. It is aimed at people who are self-employed and micro businesses.

- The **ALL-SINGING-AND-DANCING PRODUCT** adds interworking and networking capabilities. It is aimed at small businesses who want to share information and departments in large companies.

All these versions are actually one product and are sub-sets of the top-end network version. The user can unlock features with a small charge without the company being directly involved. So once the user has installed the free version the company gets sales without any additional costs.

Another way to do the same sort of thing is to bundle another product with your existing product so you'll sell more. For example, during the hay fever season, pharmaceutical companies put an anti-histamine together with a balm and a pack of paper tissues to create a special product for people who suffer from hay fever. This is called **BUNDLING** and is a good way to sell your product to non-users in your existing market. Sometimes you can supply your product to another company who will bundle it with one of their own. This is why you get a free packet of washing powder when you buy a washing machine.

You just need to spot the opportunity and sell the idea to the other company.

CONVINCING YOUR COMPETITORS' USERS TO SWITCH

This is the hardest way to grow as it often means a head-to-head battle. Not easy if they're one of the big players. You will find it cheaper and easier to attack the small-fry such as small and local businesses that don't have the strength to defend themselves or to fight back hard. This is how many of the brewery companies grew in the UK. They did it through domination – they either acquired small local companies by purchasing them, or they just drove them out of business.

In wars there are four types of attack – **FRONTAL**, **FLANKING**, **ENCIRCLEMENT** and **GUERILLA**.

- **THE FULL FRONTAL ATTACK.** Unless you have a better product at a lower price and very deep pockets, this is almost suicidal. For a full frontal attack the aggressor has to both out-gun and outnumber its rival if it's going to win. Over the years there have been many examples of

TOBY AND OLIVER RICHMOND OF SERVICING STOP *(see p39) felt they had identified the key reason for the speed with which their business was taking off. They figured that the timing was working in their favour: as customers in a period of recession sought cheaper options to servicing their vehicles at the main dealerships. They therefore wanted to capitalize on this opportunity by cornering as large a section of the market as they could as quickly as possible, using price as the incentive; they would then seek to hang on to their clients through the quality of their service.*

companies trying and failing to do this. But there are also some exceptions. In 1985 the BBC wanted a new soap opera to go directly head-to-head with ITV's very successful Coronation Street. It came up with Eastenders, which featured gritty storylines rather than the more mundane births, deaths and marriages that ran in Coronation Street. Later the BBC tackled some very hard-hitting issues such as HIV and rape. The viewing figures for Eastenders now hover around its rival's. Sometimes they're a bit less, sometimes a bit more.

- **THE FLANKING ATTACK.** This is where you attack your rival's weakest point. In business it's often about selling into markets or territories in which your rival is very weak. For example, pub chain Wetherspoons recently extended its opening hours into the early morning to offer breakfast. This was a flanking attack against McDonald's and other local cafés. Another common approach is to launch a new product that attacks one of your rival's that has reached the decline stage anyway.

- **ENCIRCLE AND ATTACK.** This is the 'blitzkrieg' from the Second World War, or 'surge' as the Americans call it nowadays. You attack on many fronts at once with new products, price cuts and aggressive marketing campaigns. Your objective is to overwhelm your rival, but you will still need very deep pockets and a weak rival to be successful.

- **A GUERILLA CAMPAIGN.** This is a swift and sudden attack on a competitor. What you must do is hit them when they least expect it, and then retreat. You have to use things like selective price cuts, local sales blitzes, short-lived marketing promotions and legal attacks on their patents and trademarks. The aim of guerilla tactics is to drain your rival's resources and grind them down.

Of course most companies have developed a defence strategy to stop other people taking their market share. For example, Unilever, Colgate Palmolive and Proctor & Gamble sell their toothpastes in many different sizes and styles to capture as many customers as possible.

"BUSINESS HAS ONLY TWO FUNCTIONS – MARKETING AND INNOVATION"

MILAN KUNDERA, CZECH-BORN WRITER

The shampoo market is the same. One of their objectives is to command more shelf space in the supermarkets and pharmacies, so it's hard for a competitor to move into the market.

Of course, you are probably small, fast and flexible. So you can easily attack a competitor's weak spot. This will be either in the competitor's product range or in the markets it serves. In this way you won't have to make a full frontal attack on their business.

To identify potential places to attack them you will need to spend time looking at each of your competitors. It's probably easier to do this with a small 'hit team' who can research the things you initially identify.

Start by looking at the following aspects for each of your rivals:

- **PRODUCT RANGE AND PRICING STRUCTURE**
- **THE MARKETS THEY SERVE AND HOW THEY SELL**
- **WHERE EACH OF THEIR PRODUCTS IS ON THE PRODUCT LIFE CYCLE**
- **THEIR STRENGTHS AND WEAKNESSES**
- **GAPS IN THEIR PRODUCT RANGE**
- **PARTS OF THE MARKET THAT THEY DON'T ADDRESS**

HAVING WORKED IN THE CALL CENTRE MARKET FOR MANY YEARS, TRUECALL'S STEVE SMITH
(Series 7) knew a lot about the competition to his product – a device for screening incoming calls and 'zapping' all nuisance and automated communications. The competition was provided by telecoms companies as services, such as anonymous caller rejection and a way for customers to block up to 10 specific numbers. A service may be more appealing to the consumer than an additional product, but the services didn't offer the same level of screening as Steve's machine, which could block 500 numbers. He pointed out that about a million people were using such services in the UK, spending about £50 per annum to do so. So, even though the trueCall product seemed expensive initially (retailing at around £100), it represented good value in the long run. That meant, with the right marketing, Steve could compete on performance and value.

Large companies are often blinkered. They become complacent and fail to see what sticks out a mile to everyone else. It's the small, fast and flexible companies that spot the opportunities which later everyone says were obvious.

For example, when Canon entered the UK photocopy market in the 1990s it didn't attack Xerox head on. It ignored the office market for large copiers and instead went for small businesses with a low-priced product. This was almost maintenance free and aimed at the small volume user.

"SOMETIMES WE STARE SO LONG AT A DOOR THAT IS CLOSING THAT WE SEE TOO LATE THE ONE THAT IS OPEN "

ALEXANDER GRAHAM BELL (1847–1922),
INVENTOR OF THE TELEPHONE

SUMMARY

Customers are the life blood of every business. To survive you must evolve and grow by attracting more and more of them. If you stand still you could end up like the Swiss watch manufacturers who failed to embrace the new quartz technology in 1970. Eight years later the sales of quartz watches overtook mechanical ones and decimated their industry. Almost two-thirds of the Swiss watch manufacturers went out of business over that period.

You need to accept what you are good at and in which part of the Product Life Cycle you prefer to operate. Then you need to decide your underlying strategy for growth – market or product development. It's best to do a bit of both with the emphasis changing according to what products you have in your development pipeline.

When you go for market share you should attack your rivals at their weakest points. These will be in their product range and the parts of the market that they don't serve. If you spend time studying your rivals and the market in which you all operate, you will spot the opportunities for growth.

TRUNKI

Rob Law appeared on Dragons' Den in Series 3 with his Trunki ride-on travel cases for children. Although he didn't receive investment from the Dragons, the Trunki cases have gone on to sell very well, with turnover trebling in the three years since he appeared in the Den. With the brand growing in strength and market penetration reaching out internationally, Rob obtained funds from a private equity investor in order to develop and promote a broader range of travel products.

Rob explains how they went about developing the range: "We enlisted the help of some of my design friends and ran a workshop to look at other opportunities in the market. In half a day we came up with over

THE TRAVEL TOY BOX *was a design by Joe, Trunki's first Chief Designer.*

300 ideas. These were then grouped in 20 categories which were then narrowed down to 10 by looking at easy wins and those that met the business strategy. Those 10 were shown at a consumer focus group, where valuable feedback was given by parents who travel with their children. Some ideas were thrown out and others refined, and from the original

300 ideas, we brought three to market. Each has been a massive success."

Rob and the Trunki team repeated the process a year later. Some concepts were a big hit with the focus groups, but to develop them fully would require a larger team. So Rob expanded the design team again and they helped launch products such as BoostApak (a car seat that doubles up as a backpack) and the Trunki Travel Toy Box.

Rob was also keen to look at the products from the sales perspective: "It was important to involve retailers early on in this process, as bringing the products to market at the right price point and through a well-considered supply chain was key to their success."

Trunki currently export to 62 countries and have 16 distributors building the brand globally.

THE ORIGINAL TRUNKI *children's suitcase (above) and one of the newer products, the BoostApak backpack-cum-car seat (below).*

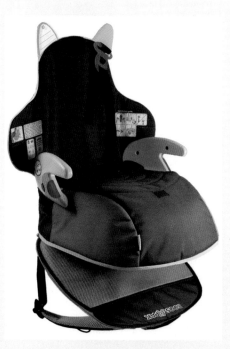

COMMANDMENT 3

FIND NEW MARKETS

Have you spotted all the gaps?

IT'S USUALLY EASIER TO SEE where a marketplace is saturated (i.e. where there are many businesses struggling to compete with each other for the same clients and customers) than to work out where the marketplace is underdeveloped. This chapter helps you identify the latter by looking at certain areas that can be exploited in many markets – geographic gaps, product gaps, price gaps, channel gaps, business model gaps and brand or lifestyle gaps.

HUW GWYTHER *appeared in the first series of the Dragons' Den, seeking investment in his publishing company, Visual Talent, which was hoping to launch a new luxury lifestyle magazine. Huw's vision was for a magazine that would have an international flavour and showcase stylish consumer goods and feature articles relating to music, film, fashion and design. Its USP would be its position: aiming for a cross-gender audience in a market that is traditionally sex specific. Huw obtained £175,000 investment from Peter Jones in return for a 40% equity stake and launched* Wonderland *magazine in 2005. In a highly competitive market,* Wonderland *has prospered and the magazine now has a circulation of 55,000. Visual Talent has also launched a new men's magazine,* Man About Town, *and is on the cusp of unleashing its third publication,* Rollacoaster.

Before we look at ways to find new markets for your product, we need to agree a definition for a **'MARKET'**. The formal description is a group of potential customers who have one or two common characteristics. So your market could be as broadly encompassing as 'all males between the age of 30 and 60 in Europe', or as narrowly limiting as, for example, 'the handful of companies that operate the railways in England'.

The key phrase is **COMMON CHARACTERISTICS**. You must clearly define what these are and the market that you reach – we call this your **SERVED MARKET**. If you don't, you'll waste a lot of your budget and effort. For example, if your product is for women over the age of 16 but you sell it only in Britain, your served market is 'women in Britain over the age of 16'. Other potential markets that you could serve would be all adult females in Europe and elsewhere in the world.

Rather than aiming for new customers outside your home territory, however, it's usually easier and cheaper to look at other groups within your own existing market or that of your competitors. These are known as **SEGMENTS** and are just more characteristics that are common between people or companies.

For example, the crowded toothpaste market has a mass of different products of all shapes and sizes. An average-sized supermarket will stock over 70 different packs and brands that take up two four-foot racks with six shelves on each. That's 48 linear feet of shelf space. The market is everyone who cleans their teeth, and the products include children's toothpastes, family versions and specialist ones for people like smokers. Each of these serve a particular segment, although there'll be some overlap.

You need to break down your overall market in a similar way with smaller and smaller segments according to four factors.

1   **DEMOGRAPHICS.** If you sell to consumers this is their sex, age and where they live. For businesses it is the company size and the location of its head office.

2   **CHARACTERISTICS.** In consumer markets this is their income, background, education, occupation, number of

children, etc. For businesses it is the industry and their structure, such as plc or private company.

3 **LIFESTYLE.** For consumers this is their interests and activities outside work. It's also what other types of product they use and which brands. For businesses it's their buying habits – how often they make a purchase and how much they spend.

4 **PERSONALITY.** If you sell to consumers this covers whether they are sociable and what aspirations they have. For companies, it's how they actually make the decision to purchase a product. For example, they could go for multiple tenders or they could use preferred suppliers.

Think of your ideal customer, or typical customer, and describe them according to the characteristics above. Then make a similar list for each of the competitors that operate in your overall market. If you do this as a matrix on a large sheet of paper, you'll see the parts of the market that could be potential opportunities. These will fall into one of six areas which are called **GAPS**. They are geographic, product, price, channel, business model and lifestyle.

You need to identify one or two of these gaps or niches that are small enough to be of limited interest to your competitors but large enough to be profitable for you. It's an added bonus if they also have some growth potential.

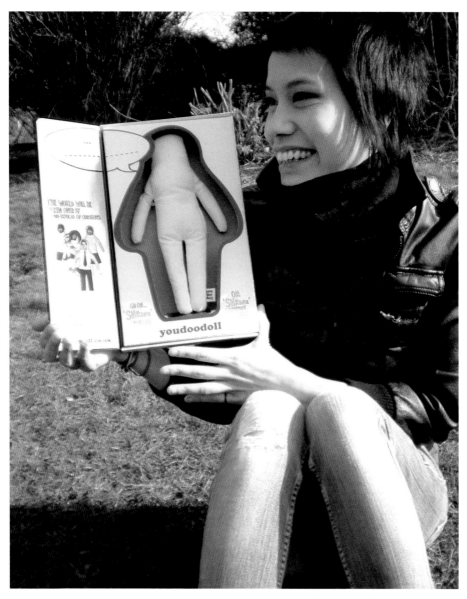

SARAH LU'S YOUDOO DOLLS *(see pp184–5) had started to sell well in the UK, but with the onset of the recession in 2009 sales slowed over the prime Christmas period. Sarah Lu had already begun to tap into foreign markets, but, with a weak pound, this was now the best time to push on the export front. In February of 2010, Youdoo signed up with a US distributor and by spring were in talks with similar companies in Australia and Japan.*

"THE MARKET IS SPLIT INTO EVER-MULTIPLYING, EVER-CHANGING SETS OF MICRO-MARKETS THAT DEMAND A CONTINUALLY EXPANDING RANGE OF OPTIONS " ALVIN TOFFLER, SOCIAL COMMENTATOR

GEOGRAPHIC GAP

The geographic gaps are the easiest to spot (i.e. are there territories outside of your current area that are ripe for exploitation?) but often such gaps can be logistically difficult to get to and costly to serve. There are some issues that you must consider before you decide to market your products outside your home territory:

- **COMPETITORS.** You must identify and analyse all the competition that currently operates in each of your geographic markets and estimate their commitment to it. It's not very wise to attack a competitor head on when they have invested a tremendous amount of time and money in that particular market.

- **CULTURES AND ATTITUDES.** People use and purchase products for different reasons in different social groups and cultures. This is often overlooked, but for instance British products with a Union Jack emblazoned on the packaging do not go down very well in France.

- **LANGUAGE AND LEGISLATION.** If you're looking at other countries, you may have to translate any operating instructions, warranty information and packaging into each foreign language. You must also consider the Consumer Protection legislation and other legal aspects for each different country you want to serve.

You really must address all the issues above and then see if the niche still looks profitable. If it does, you need to think about how you could possibly address the market considering its location. Mail order can be an easy option and provide a relatively cheap way of testing the market.

You may need to set up a local office, especially if your new target market is overseas; in other situations you might be able to use a locally based agent or travelling sales rep. In Commandment 4 we will look at agents and other types of outlet that you might use.

PRODUCT GAP

There are always gaps in product ranges and opportunities with new technology. You can look at them from two ends. You could start with the problem and solve it with some technology, or you could come up with some new technology and then look for a problem to solve.

James Dyson famously used the first approach. He started with a problem with existing vacuum cleaners and devised new technology to create a top-of-the-range product. This stimulated the market and forced other manufacturers onto their back foot. The problem was vacuum cleaners lost suction when the bag started to fill up. He therefore designed a new product with new technology to fill the gap.

THE ANYWAY SPRAY *(above) for use in household sprays and aerosol cans and Butterfly Technology's* **SQUEEZE WITH EASE GADGET FOR TUBES** *(below) had several similarities in terms of what they offered and their market position. In both cases a problem had been identified and a solution devised and developed. Also in both cases there was a clear benefit to the end user: in fact both products served the function of getting every last drop of product out of their respective containers. However, the problem was that, again in both cases, their customer would not be the end user but the manufacturers of tube dispensers and spray cans. That meant that there needed to be a clear benefit to the manufacturers.*

FOR THE SQUEEZE WITH EASE *it was difficult to see what the benefit would be: the tube would need to be longer or contain less product to accommodate the device, which in itself would be an additional bit of plastic that would need to be manufactured and inserted into the tube. It would therefore cost more and use more plastic.*

THE CRUCIAL FACTOR IN MICHAEL PRITCHARD'S ANYWAY SPRAY PITCH *was that its technology meant that aerosol cans could use it in combination with compressed air rather than a gas such as butane or propane, meaning a saving in gas and a much easier process for recycling, which, again, would have cost benefits.*

Universities and research organizations often do it the other way round. They start by creating some piece of new technology and then look for a problem to solve or an existing product to improve.

Sometimes the gap is an existing product that can be adapted to a particular market segment. Take the mobile phone business, which is driven by price and performance. Every new model adds more features, is smaller and is cheaper or the same price. However, this strategy tends to disenfranchise older people who can't manage the small keys and just want a simple phone. Recently two small manufacturers spotted this gap and now supply simple mobile phones with big keys and large text display. These are aimed specifically at the 'older people' segment of the market.

Another way to fill the product gap is to find a large company that has something missing from their product range. You could then approach them to offer your product badged under their own brand name. In this case you would be called an **OEM** (Original Equipment Manufacturer). The computer industry is renowned for this approach. Many computer monitors are actually designed and

A GREAT MANY COMPUTER PERIPHERALS *start off as quite expensive products and then come down in price as more and more manufacturers catch up with the technology. David and Patti Bailey of Motormouse felt that some consumers would be prepared to pay a premium for something a little different to your everyday computer mouse. They styled theirs as top-end sports cars. Other, more gimmicky car-mice had gone before, but in this case the mouse would be exquisitely detailed, with opening boots and quality paintwork, and have the best wireless operational system available. Recognizing that this is a niche market, economically speaking, the Baileys are going for as wide a distribution as possible and are using onboard airline sales as a way to get a foothold in overseas markets.*

manufactured by specialist companies or TV manufacturers and then badged by the computer companies. This means that you'll find the same monitor used across many different brands.

PRICE GAP

Again this is easy to spot and we alluded to it in the previous chapter. It's when you produce slightly different versions of an existing product at different price points: cheap, luxury, etc.

The low-cost airlines such as Ryanair and easyJet built their businesses on the gap left by the larger carriers' original price model. British Airways responded in 1998 with a wholly-owned subsidiary called Go Fly. For the first couple of years it suffered mounting losses and was sold as a management buyout in 2001.

Supermarkets do the same thing with their own label products, which they brand under a 'value range'.

As we saw before, software companies and car manufacturers fill the price gaps with their own products to keep out the competition. So do the FMCG (fast-moving consumer goods) companies with different packs such as the 'family size'.

CHANNEL GAP

Sometimes you can identify a gap in the market that you or others don't serve with existing sales methods, whether it's through the internet or a retail outlet. In other words, there's a market segment that you don't address because people can't buy your products.

For example, The Book People company has a partnership with the Puffin Book Club to sell children's books to families who might otherwise rarely go into bookshops. Agents send the Puffin Book Club catalogues to schools; the schools distribute the catalogues to parents in return for a percentage of the total sales price of the bulk order.

CLIVE BILLING NOTICED A CHANNEL GAP *in the online jewellery retail market. Though he already had an online business of this kind, he studied similar businesses and noticed how a key competitor was producing huge revenues in the lower, 'click-and-buy' end of the market. That's when he decided that a freshly branded site was needed for this sector of the market. See how this plan came to fruition on pp64–5.*

SHANE LAKE AND TONY CHARLES *of the Hungryhouse website appeared in Series 5 of Dragons' Den with a new business model for the UK takeaway market. The marketing for takeaways tends to be via competing mail shots posted through people's doors for local restaurants and kitchens. Shane and Tony's idea was to create a single website into which a consumer would type their location and then be offered a range of takeaway options to choose from. The user would be able to see the range of local takeaways and cuisine types on offer, opt for one, select from their menu and make the order online, all from one site. James and Duncan saw potential in the business model and offered the £100,000 investment needed for marketing and signing up more restaurants.*

BUSINESS MODEL GAP

Video and games rental company LoveFilm took the high street video rental model and combined it with Amazon's business model to create its business – a subscription-based DVD rental company operating via the internet.

Similarly a company in Germany offers a rental service for baby clothes. This is also subscription-based where, for a fixed monthly fee, parents rent the clothes they want and return them when the baby grows out of them.

These are just two examples of people who have adapted someone else's business model to fill a gap in their own market.

> **" YOU WILL DISCOVER GREAT RICHES ONLY WHEN YOU LOOK AT MARKETS THROUGH THE OTHER END OF THE TELESCOPE – NOT THE LENS OF WHAT YOU WANT TO SELL, BUT THE LENS OF WHAT PEOPLE WANT TO BUY "** GARY BENCIVENGA, MARKETING GURU

BRAND OR LIFESTYLE GAP

This gap is totally different. It's more about creating a lifestyle around the brand. The car manufacturers like BMW and Alfa Romeo also sell clothing, baseball caps, and toy cars, all of which are branded by the company. Football clubs do the same with their kit.

If you go into one of the mobile phone shops that have sprung up in motorway service stations, you'll find they sell covers for all makes of mobile phones. These are designed and manufactured by third parties. You can call this brand extension or add-ons. It's all about the same thing – spotting an opportunity to exploit your own or someone else's brand or market position.

SUMMARY

There are opportunities for growth all around you. They're in your existing marketplace and you will find them when you segment the market into groups of potential customers with similar characteristics. Once you have done that you must analyse the parts of the market that you and each of your competitors don't serve. You'll then easily spot the gaps that you can go on to exploit.

DIAMOND GEEZER

Clive Billing had worked in the diamond industry for 40 years and owned his own business for about 20 when he ventured into the Den, seeking an investment of £255,000. The internet business he was running, called Diamond Geezer, was profitable, but not hugely, and Clive had identified a more lucrative sector of the market.

NEGOTIATIONS *were cut short in the Den, with neither side eager to stretch across the 10% difference between the equity being offered and the equity being asked for.*

Up to this point, his best-selling items had been £1,500 engagement rings, but now he wanted to have a separate focus on the more mass-market 'click-and-buy' sector – that is, items in the region of £25–50.

The vehicle for this would be a new specialist website that would use specialist fulfilment software systems that Clive and his team had developed for the Diamond Geezer site. It would be pitched at the fashion end of the jewellery market and geared for quick and repeat online sales.

Clive's pitch offered the Dragons a share of the established business, but any cash investment was to be used exclusively in the development of the new 'click-and-buy' aspect of the two-brand business. It was a tough encounter in the Den, with the stakes raised to the highest figure ever asked for by an entrepreneur at that point. After much wrangling, James, Theo and Peter offered the money in return for 40% equity. Clive countered with a 30% offer, but the Dragons didn't bite. Negotiations ended at that point, with Clive determining to look for investment elsewhere.

When James visited Clive at his Gloucestershire premises 18 months later, it was clear that diversifying into this lower-end market had worked well. Clive had rejected 21 investment offers and pursued the business plan that he presented to the Dragons. The new click-and-buy brand, called Loving the Bead, was funded exclusively from Clive's existing business.

SALES FROM CLIVE'S *existing online business, Diamond Geezer, funded the new venture into what was for him a new sector of the jewellery market. Known as 'click-and-buy' it was based on inexpensive impulse buys and repeat sales.*

LOVING THE BEAD *now processes an average of 200 sales a day and is on target for a second year's turnover of £1.1 million with six-figure net profits.*

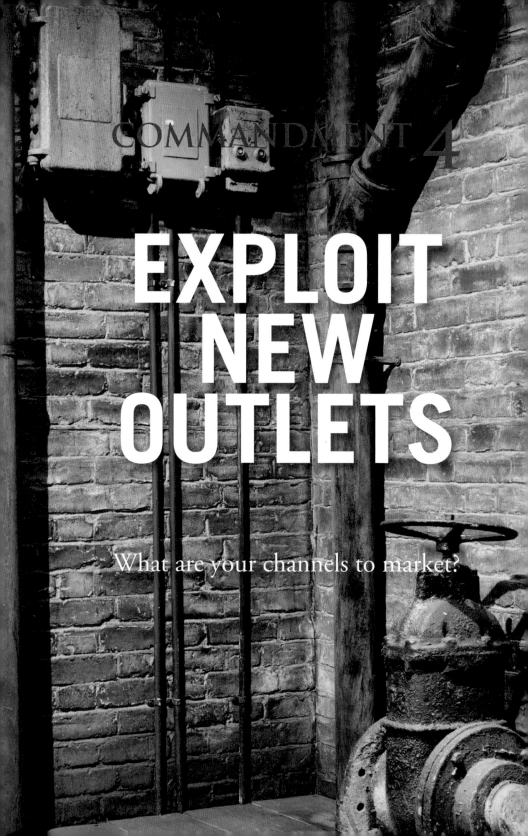

COMMANDMENT 4

EXPLOIT NEW OUTLETS

What are your channels to market?

IT'S ALL VERY WELL TO PRODUCE A GREAT PRODUCT but if no one can get hold of it you're actually wasting your time and money. Marketing people describe the outlets where your product is sold as 'channels to market'. You will almost certainly find opportunities to grow your business if you look for outlets that can be exploited alongside the ones you are already using. We look at the wide variety of options today, ranging from traditional 'glass on the street' outlets to innovative selling schemes and technology-enabled channels such as the internet.

UNDERSTAND YOUR 'CHANNELS TO MARKET'

The term 'channels to market' is a good description for your sales outlets, because selling in the broad marketplace usually involves more than one third party in a chain or channel.

For example, in your home territory you could sell to a distributor or wholesaler who would then sell your products to retailers. You might also sell direct to the national retail chains as well as large users such as central or local government. In this case you would have two channels – retail sales and direct sales.

For overseas markets, on the other hand, you would traditionally sell to an importer or agent who would supply the wholesalers in the particular country. Of course nowadays things are slightly different as with the internet you can theoretically sell your products anywhere in the world…

THINK ABOUT PRODUCT OWNERSHIP

One of the things that you must always consider is who has ownership of your product as it moves through the channels. In some channels, ownership moves from the manufacturer to each member of the channel in turn. This is always true in retail sales, except if you use agents who never own your product. It is sometimes true with internet shops like Amazon, but not always.

Ownership moves if the manufacturer or supplier sells the product to the first member of the channel at a discount off the end-user price. They then take responsibility for selling it on.

If ownership doesn't move, you are responsible for shipping your product to the end-user. Some mail order companies will ask you to drop ship the product direct to the customer so you retain

"THANK GOD WE'RE LIVING IN A COUNTRY WHERE THE SKY'S THE LIMIT, THE STORES ARE OPEN LATE AND YOU CAN SHOP IN BED THANKS TO THE INTERNET "

JOAN RIVERS, AMERICAN COMEDIENNE

ownership. In this case you will need a dispatch department which can ship to individual users as well as in bulk to wholesalers.

TRADITIONAL CHANNELS

These days most businesses use a mix of traditional channels plus technology-enabled channels such as the internet. This allows them to serve as much of the market as possible.

Here is a list of traditional channels and things you need to bear in mind with each one.

- **'GLASS ON THE STREETS'.** Traditional shops, supermarkets and market stalls are known in marketing as 'glass on the streets'. There are many parties involved when you sell through such outlets, and everyone in the chain wants a percentage of the sales price. You therefore have to give wholesalers a discount off the end-user price, plus bonuses for any extra volumes they create. Companies who operate through a traditional distribution channel often use a separate sales force to help drive their products through the channel. In some cases these salespeople also deal with the large mail order companies. They might also be responsible for sales agents and merchandisers (see below).

- **DIRECT SALES.** Many companies employ a direct sales force that will sell direct to large organizations such as local and central government as well as major supermarkets or retail chains rather than going through a third party wholesaler. The key issue here is conflict and competition, e.g. different volume pricing structures, between the direct sales force and other channels whether they are the traditional ones or on the internet.

- **SALES AGENTS.** Many small companies operating in the arts and crafts market, for example, will use freelance sales agents. These people travel round selling to the small independent shops and specialist outlets such as the visitor centres in stately homes. Each sales agent will typically handle four or five different product ranges from different manufacturers. In this way they can improve their chances of making a sale at each visit. They take an order from the retailer on behalf of the manufacturer who drop ships the goods directly to the outlet. The sales agent is paid a monthly commission, and ownership does not pass from the manufacturer to the agent.

MICHAEL LEA OF EARLE'S *(see pp212–13) is an example of a van-based business, in this case supplying hot and cold snacks and ice creams to local businesses in the northwest of England.*

- **VAN SALES.** Rather than losing a massive amount of margin to wholesalers some companies prefer to take the shop to the customer. In the consumer field this includes outlets like the ice cream van and travelling fishmonger who sets up a van in a different pub car park every day of the week. In industry it includes the tool companies and suppliers of industrial consumables who regularly visit garages and workshops around their individual territories. They take orders from the workshop manager and will either supply the products from the back of the van or send the order to the company who will then drop ship them to the customer. The company then sends an invoice to the customer. Van sales are either directly employed by the company, operated as a franchise or set up as an independent outlet.

- **VALUE ADDED RESELLERS (VARS).** This type of outlet first appeared in the late 1980s with the rise of the personal computer and associated software. VARs are third parties who will take your product and combine it with another to create a new product with a larger value that they sell on. In other words they add value to products. Typically VARs are software companies that sell 'vertical market' applications, in other words a complete package that combines hardware and software. Another example of the Value Added Reseller is the vehicle tracking systems that incorporate mobile phones and GPS technology from third parties. The vehicle tracking suppliers create extra value by combining these products with their own software and installation services.

- **JOINT VENTURES.** There will be other non-competing companies who sell into your target market. You can identify these if you ask yourself, "what other products do customers in my target market use?" The answer can sometimes lead to two companies working together to sell each other's products, or to jointly create a new product aimed at their common market.

- **MERCHANDISERS.** In some industries a company will supply a display stand for its products in a specialist outlet. This is usually done on a sale or return basis, in other words ownership of the product does not pass to

THE MAGIC WHITEBOARD COMPANY, *which featured in Series 6 of Dragons' Den, began as a mail order business that used its own internet shop for marketing the product. Having secured investment from the Den, Magic Whiteboards are now also selling through many retail chains, including Staples, Boots and Ryman. It has been one of the most successful ventures from the Den.*

the outlet. Often the merchandiser rents the space and pays a small commission. At other times it just pays a larger commission on each sale. It is the merchandiser's job to regularly visit the outlet, check how many items have been sold and replenish the stock. The company then sends an invoice to the outlet for the price of the goods less commission.

• **MAIL ORDER.** Any small company that wants to extend its reach beyond its local area has to consider mail order in its many forms. You could build a database yourself, produce your own catalogue and send it out. But that requires specialist skills so it is better to sub-contract this to a professional firm. As an alternative you could place your product with one of the many existing mail order catalogue companies, such as Scots of Stow and Lakeland. The main issue with mail order is the high possibility of returns, because it is a channel where the customer doesn't get a chance to touch the product before buying. Always factor in for the cost of returns with mail order. Also bear in mind that nowadays most companies also use the internet for mail order in the same way they might have used printed catalogues in the past. They supplement their website with flyers through the post that contain special offers and loyalty discounts.

- **CATALOGUE SALES.** Don't confuse this channel with mail order. Catalogue sales involve a freelance distributor delivering a catalogue to a home or business, returning a few days later to collect the catalogue and the orders. The following week they deliver the goods and collect payment. In effect these people are freelance sales agents who work on a commission-only basis.

- **'OFF THE PAGE' SALES.** Some companies very successfully sell directly through advertising in newspapers, magazines and other publications. This is known as 'selling off the page' and is a very specialist form of mail order advertising. It is particularly useful to reach people

SHOES GALORE *(see pp 100–1)*
uses a party plan method to
sell women's shoes. It's a versatile
sales method, popular mainly
with women who can work
around other commitments
and combine sales work with
a social gathering.

who can't access your website or refuse to buy via the internet because of security fears. You often see 'off the page' advertisements in the Saturday and Sunday newspapers, as the weekend is when people have the time to browse. Your product might catch their eye when they didn't even know it existed or that they needed it.

- **PARTY PLANS.** In the 1950s a woman called Brownie Wise invented the famous system of party plan sales for Tupperware. Today many companies use the system to sell things like kitchen products, greetings cards, jewellery, cosmetics and lingerie. It involves women inviting their friends to a party in their home where they demonstrate and sell products. It's primarily about a fun social environment that is also an opportunity to sell goods that are aimed at women.

THE FIT FUR LIFE COMPANY *(see pp138–9) makes regular appearances at dog shows, such as Crufts, with its specially designed canine treadmills. In fact, the company has set up a team dedicated to showing and selling the products at the various dog-related trade and consumer exhibitions throughout the UK. They also attend similar events in Europe, including InterZoo in Germany and the World Dog Show in Denmark.*

- **THEMED FAIRS AND SHOWS.** Just about every weekend somewhere around the country there will be a wedding fair, carpet sale, craft show or some other themed fair. Nowadays there are even divorce fairs. They're all opportunities to market and sell your products or services to a specific segment of your market. So for example if you sell wills and lasting powers of attorney you should attend wedding fairs and divorce fairs because that's where you will find your target market.

TECHNOLOGY-ENABLED CHANNELS

The advent of the internet and mobile devices has opened up massive opportunities for companies to grow outside their home markets and reduce sales costs. Indeed, many organizations such as Amazon, Late Rooms and LoveFilm are absolutely reliant on the technology-enabled channels.

Traditional channels that use 'glass on the streets' or other fixed assets such as vans will continue to exist alongside online channels. One reason for them to endure is because there's human contact during the sale, which is an opportunity to set up and build customer relationships. Consumers can also see and touch the product before they buy which gives them a sense of security. On the other hand, the success of online shops such as Amazon and Apple's iTunes store, which has contributed to the decline of high street bookshops and CD/DVD chains, shows that lower pricing of a broader range of products is probably more important to consumers of certain products than the opportunity to see and touch them.

INTERNET SHOPS

Nowadays there aren't many reasons why any company in the consumer market shouldn't have its own internet shop or shopping cart in various places on the internet. There are four issues that you must consider, however, before you go down the internet route:

1 **SLOW BROADBAND.** Some of your potential customers may not have a fast broadband service or any internet access at all. This is particularly true if you sell to people in rural areas, disadvantaged groups and the elderly.

2 **A PICTURE MAY NOT BE ENOUGH.** Your product may be such that customers want to touch and feel it before they buy. Products like shoes, clothes and non-branded foods can fall into this category.

3 **RELUCTANCE TO PAY ONLINE.** Especially if your product has a high price, many people may be reluctant to risk using their credit card without checking that you are a bona fide company.

4 **DEALING WITH RETURNS.** With products such as clothes you should expect a high rate of returns. These will cost you money and will need to be correctly handled.

SELLING THROUGH EBAY AND AMAZON

Many companies have an internet shop on their own website and also sell through other shopping sites, especially Amazon and/or eBay, which charge a fee for each sale.

A vast number of micro-businesses are run from home that sell only through eBay; some even have sales of around £1 million per annum. eBay only ever acts as an agent and never has ownership of the product whether it's sold through auction or at a fixed price.

Amazon works as a channel in two ways. First, as a traditional seller it buys from publishers and other manufacturers for its own stock. Secondly, it acts as an agent taking a commission on other suppliers' books, DVDs, toys, computers and other goods listed on its marketplace.

SELLING THROUGH OTHER ONLINE CHANNELS

- **RESERVATION SITES.** Traditionally hotels sold rooms through travel agents, tour operators, accommodation agencies and the airlines. But nowadays there are many online companies providing a central reservation service for hotels, holidays, concerts, and so on. They allow the suppliers to extend their reach in exchange for a small sales commission.

- **PRICE COMPARISON SITES.** In the past insurance brokers and financial advisers worked from offices on the high street or as freelancers from home. Today they have heavy competition in the form of price comparison sites on the internet. These just act as agents and take a commission on every sale and renewal.

- **BUYING GROUPS.** These used to be known as cooperatives where groups of individuals, such as farmers, would

HUNGRYHOUSE *(see also p62) follows the reservation site model – it provides a central hub from which to order takeaway meals from restaurants local to the user's area. It is free to use for customers, while the restaurants that sign up to the service pay a commission on orders taken through the site.*

get together to buy in bulk. This allowed them to take advantage of volume discounts. Today it's all internet-based and known as group buying or team buying. The team members, who do not necessarily know each other, use the internet site as a way to buy in bulk. In the same way as eBay the site takes a small commission for every transaction.

MOBILE PHONE CHANNELS

On a final note about the technology-enabled channels, in the developed world almost everyone has a mobile phone, some even have two: one personal and one for work. These days you can exploit mobile phone technology to sell car parking, rail tickets, cinema seats and lots more using SMS messaging or the phones' inbuilt internet browsers. You can also create your own App that will enable users to buy your product of service direct from their mobile device.

" CHANNELS DO NOT STAND STILL. NEW INSTITUTIONS AND ORGANIZATIONS EMERGE, AND NEW CHANNEL SYSTEMS EVOLVE. " PHILIP KOTLER, MARKETING GURU

PROMOTIONAL SALES CHANNELS

Sometimes a promotional tool also works as a sales channel. Exhibitions or shows fall into this category if you sell products off your stand. Whilst the schemes below should never be a primary sales channel, they will allow you to reach markets you wouldn't normally get to. They also help to promote your company and its products. But they need to be managed so you don't damage your reputation and the resultant backlash from the people involved in the scheme.

- **USER-GET-USER SCHEMES.** American Express has a referral system which is a very effective way to increase its membership. Whilst it's more of a promotional scheme than a sales channel, commission does change hands in the form of a voucher system or credit. This has to be managed because of the knock-on effect on your reputation if you get it wrong.

- **AFFILIATE SCHEMES.** Amazon, for example, has a referral system that allows other websites to create links to products on its own site. This is called an affiliate scheme and the referring site receives a small commission on every sale made through the link. Companies such as webgains.com and clickbank.com offer a facility where you can sign up as a merchant and offer an affiliate scheme just like Amazon.

- **MEMBERSHIP GROUPS.** Golf clubs, Chambers of Commerce and other membership groups may like to sell your product to their members. They expect a sales commission and discount for their members as this increases the perceived value of membership.

WHY HAVE MORE THAN ONE CHANNEL?

Most companies use a mix of sales channels so they can serve the widest market possible. The more channels you use, the more customers you will reach. But there are two challenges. One is to identify which channels will be the most cost effective and the other is to manage the channels so they don't compete with each other. Sometimes they can absorb too much management time and effort.

SAMANTHA FOUNTAIN, *who appeared in Series 2 of the Den, has revised her strategy for selling her Shewee products (see p34): "Initially, I didn't want to sell on the internet at all, not even on Shewee.com [because of the extra admin involved]. However, the advice from Dragons' Den was to get it on my website so people could get hold of the product. I wanted to sell only to high street retailers, as these would be the companies investing in sales efforts and marketing. We have recently introduced a policy to sell only to high street retailers and websites that target particular market areas. We no longer sell to people or companies that sell on eBay or Amazon."*

Direct Wines, based in Reading, is an example of a company exploiting a mix of sales channels. It runs a number of different branded wine companies that sell through mail order, the internet and high street shops. These include Laithwaites, Virgin Wines, the Wall Street Journal Wine Club and the Sunday Times Wine Club. The company also has 11 wine shops on the high street under the Laithwaite brand. So each segment of users is served by a different brand, although often through the same mail order channel. In this way Direct Wines has cornered a significant proportion of the overall wine market in the UK. It has also made inroads into America with its Wall Street Journal Club.

GUY PORTELLI

Guy offered an interesting approach to his selling channels. Having worked as a sculptor for many years he was familiar with the percentage that galleries take on sales, which can be 50% or more. In fairness to galleries, sales can be infrequent, rents are often high and they spend a lot of time and money on marketing to attract buyers to their showrooms. However, for a new series of works, Guy decided to circumvent the gallery's cut by hiring a prestigious gallery himself – the Mall Galleries in London.

To raise the funds for hiring the space and producing the work, he pitched his proposal to the Dragons, offering 25% of sales for the entire series. In compensation for the marketing

GUY TOOK HIS PORTRAIT OF GRACE JONES *into the Den to woo the Dragons.*

that a gallery would normally provide, Guy reckoned on the Dragons' contacts to produce sufficient interest in the exhibition, as well as the work's subject matter of course: pop idols, including Grace Jones, the Spice Girls and Bob Marley. Theo, Peter and James went for the deal, offering £80,000 for a shared 25% stake.

WHERE CUSTOMERS WILL BUY

The way you think about which of your channels to use comes from the market segments that you want to serve. For each segment you need to ask yourself "where will these customers prefer to buy?" It might be in the comfort of their own home via mail order or the internet. It might be from a specialist retailer or a supermarket.

You must think about the customer first rather than how you would prefer to sell your product. Sometimes it's fairly obvious, other times it just needs a bit of common sense. For instance, an internet shop using high-quality photographs and videos of your products is probably no good if you want to get to users in rural communities because many of your target customers would not have high-speed internet access.

One of the best ways to discover where your target customers would prefer to buy is to ask them. When you've identified your target market segment, you should prepare a questionnaire and organize a survey through the post or through a focus group.

ORGANIZING A FOCUS GROUP

For a focus group you will need to invite a dozen or so people from your target market to a two-hour discussion. When you've got them together you should explain the various channels that you could use and ask the group to discuss them. Your aim is to end up with a list of their preferred channels in preference order. If you record and transcribe their discussions, you'll also get some valuable insights into the way people like to shop for your type of product and where they would expect to find it.

MANAGE YOUR CHANNELS

With selling channels you get a situation called **PUSH AND PULL**. When you use a third party to sell you potentially lose control of your sales, so you will have to spend time and money 'pushing' your products through the channel. You will also have to promote your products to the market so potential customers 'pull' the products through the channel. With a large number of different outlets this can take up a significant amount of management time and effort.

You have to realize that your sales costs are directly proportional to the size of the market you serve and the number of channels you use. Some of these costs are relatively easy to calculate, while others are more difficult.

- **MARGIN COSTS.** The more third parties you have in a channel, the more margin you will have to sacrifice. If you sell direct, you keep all the margin for yourself. If you sell to wholesalers, they would expect a discount of around 40% to 50%. If you also employ an importer they would also need a percentage of the margin. So although your sales quantities will increase, your sales value won't rise by the same proportion.

- **RESOURCE COSTS.** You will have to serve each channel with people who take orders and despatch your products. In some cases it could be the same people, but for other channels you may need a separate sales force. You must also realize that different channels have different expectations on delivery. The wholesaler, for instance, would not necessarily expect next-day delivery whereas for an end user it's almost mandatory these days.

- **MARKETING COSTS.** You will have to promote your products to 'pull' them through the channel. In some cases you will need separate literature for each channel. For example, a wholesaler needs a trade price list and maybe detailed technical specifications. Whereas a retailer needs glossy literature rather than specifications. You will also have to run special incentive promotions to 'push' products through the channel. These take time to develop and then more effort to promote to each of the channel members.

- **RETURNS COSTS.** You will always get additional 'returns' if you use a channel where the customer cannot directly see and touch your product before they buy. Many companies count these as warranty costs and resell them as seconds through a specialist channel such as market traders or eBay.

- **MANAGEMENT COSTS.** Finally there is a hidden cost of management time and accounting effort. One of the most common problems is competition between two or more channels. For instance, your direct sales force can offer a better discount than a distributor, which can lead to a nasty argument if they both try and sell to the same customer.

ED WRAY'S BARBESKEW, *which featured in Series 6, obtained a lot of its early sales through independent garden centres that didn't want to stretch themselves to the minimum order quantities set by major barbecue manufacturers. Ed's business struggled through the first couple of years, but is now running profitably. As Ed says: "BarbeSkew has now passed its third birthday – something that most new businesses fail to do. In 2009, it posted a quarter of a million pound turnover and has gained some esteemed customers, including the Next Directory and Notcutts, one of the oldest garden centres in the UK. The business has now passed its break even point, is starting to make a profit and looks set to have a firm foothold in the UK's barbecue market for many years to come."*

SUMMARY

Nowadays with so many channels to market there is almost too much choice and you must make sure that you don't spread your marketing efforts too thin. Always start with the customer and market and find out how and where they would prefer to buy your products. Be careful of costs because sometimes they can outweigh the additional sales the channel produces. Often this is difficult to calculate and a great deal of management time can be spent on channels that actually lose you money.

PARAGON PE

When Paul Ward stepped into the Den in Series 7, his company, Paragon PE, had been trading for three years, selling anti-microbial cleaning products into the commercial market. At the time, the company had a turnover of about £450,000 and a profit of £190,000. He went to the Dragons offering just 5% equity in exchange for £100,000 investment. These funds would be used to help launch the company's new product, Halo, an antimicrobial laundry detergent aimed at the consumer retail market. As Paul freely admitted, his company had

THE DETERGENT *that Paul wanted to launch in the domestic market.*

been fortunate in capitalizing on the sudden increased demand for antibacterial, antifungal and antiviral products, at a time when the UK was gripped by the prospect of a swine flu epidemic. Their kind of products were in high demand, and Paul wanted to pursue this demand into the domestic market. However, he had set himself a tight negotiating threshold. He had offered 5% equity and it emerged that he would go no higher than 10%. The closest any of the Dragons came to meeting this was with James's offer of the money for a staggered return. He would initially take a 30% stake in the business, but this would reduce to 10% over three years if Paul met his projected targets (£250,000 profit in the first year after investment, £500,000 in the following year and £750,000 profit in the year after that).

Paul felt that the deal was too much weighted towards James. For good or bad, Paul stuck to the limit he had originally set, and says: "I do believe if I had taken James Caan's offer the product range would be selling into retail but

PARAGON'S CORE RANGE *of cleaning products are aimed at the commercial market.*

A STEADFAST PAUL WARD *proved as resistant as a stubborn grass stain to offers in the Den.*

at a high cost to the company." By December 2009, Paragon PE had already surpassed the Year 1 target. Paul had anticipated this, which was why he turned down James's offer.

Paragon PE has since signed a £2.4 million distribution contract to supply products into eight countries and is in the final contract stages with a plastics company in the States to supply antimicrobial plastic components. The business was recently valued at £4.2 million.

COMMANDMENT 5

CONTROL THE COSTS OF GROWTH

What is the expense of expansion?

FOR A GROWING BUSINESS, it's easy to forget the big picture and keep busy focusing on day-to-day problems and opportunities. Successful businesses, however, invest time in financial planning and regularly review financial performance in order to control the growth. If you've read the first book in this Dragons' Den series – *Start Your Own Business* – then you know the basics of accounting, such as how to calculate VAT and keep your books in order. Here, we look at more advanced ways of using budgets and calculations that will help you to predict and manage profitability and cash flow during a period of growth.

This Commandment focuses specifically on financial control. As referred to elsewhere in this book, non-financial performance measures can be equally as important in controlling a growing business. These include market share, customer loyalty, productivity, quality, and investment in research and development. Ideally financial and non-financial performance measures should be used together to provide a balanced view of a business.

WHY USE BUDGETS, RATIOS AND MEASURES?

Many small businesses produce financial reports only when they have to for their obligatory annual accounts. However, preparing and using a broader range of financial information is essential for growing businesses and helps to avoid costly ill-informed decisions. In particular, you should have a sound grasp of your cash operating cycle and regularly make cash flow forecasts when your business is growing. We will look at this later in this chapter.

Preparing and using budgets will help you manage your growing business in the following ways:

- **PLANNING AND COORDINATION.** Budgeting helps you to plan, coordinate and integrate different business activities. For example purchasing/production should be matched with sales.

- **TARGET-SETTING.** Setting motivating budget targets will help you control the direction of your business and subsequently evaluate the performance of budget holders.

- **PERFORMANCE MONITORING.** Monthly budget reports will provide a useful benchmark against which you can assess actual performance and check your business is on track to achieve its goals.

- **ALLOCATION OF RESPONSIBILITY.** Budgeting allocates responsibility for financial control to budget holders.

You should monitor your financial performance ratios as your business grows. This commandment covers three types of measures:

- **PROFITABILITY**
- **SHORT-TERM SOLVENCY AND LIQUIDITY**
- **LONG-TERM SOLVENCY AND LIQUIDITY**

We won't pretend that ratios provide answers to every question, and would stress that their interpretation can be subjective. However, they are a useful guideline to business performance and a good way of highlighting areas that need further investigation.

MEASURING AND INCREASING PROFIT

The early years of many new businesses are focused on establishing market share and growing revenue. As a business matures it needs to focus on profits to ensure its continued survival. However, profit on its own is not necessarily the best measure of success. Profit should be measured in relation to the size of the investment required to achieve that level of profit. Therefore, the best measure of profitability is **RETURN ON INVESTMENT (ROI)**, which we'll cover on the next few pages. First we show you the main ways to calculate and improve your return, then calculate and maximize your use of investment and then put them together to calculate and grow your return on investment.

IMPROVING 'RETURN'

There are two key measures of return: gross profit margin (below) and net profit margin (p97).

HOW TO CALCULATE GROSS PROFIT MARGIN

This measures the margin made on top of direct costs.

$$\text{gross profit margin \%} = \frac{\text{gross profit}}{\text{revenue}} \times 100$$

HOW TO INCREASE GROSS PROFIT MARGIN

You can improve your gross profit margin when you grow revenue and control costs. Revenue can be grown by increasing sales volume, increasing prices or, if possible, both.

- **INCREASING SALES VOLUME.** You can increase market share through marketing or discounting. Many businesses offer discounts with the aim of increasing sales volume and profits. However, the cost of the discount often outweighs the benefit of the increase in sales volume – and ends up reducing profitability. You can also explore opportunities for growth with new products and/or new markets (see Commandments 2, 3 and 4 for ideas).

TANGLE TEEZER

Shaun Pulfrey and his product, the Tangle Teezer, appeared in Series 5. He didn't get any investment from the Dragons, but when Duncan made a return visit to Shaun to see how his business was progressing, he declared that it was one of the few investments that he wished he had invested in.

IF SALES *continue as predicted, Shaun's company will soon be the biggest supplier of hair brushes to Boots in the UK.*

Like all young, product-based businesses, increasing sales was paramount for Shaun. Following his Dragons' Den appearance, online sales of the Tangle Teezer took off and Shaun soon picked up some celebrity endorsements and industry product awards, all of which helped launch the revolutionary hair brush in Boots in late 2008. Boots stocked it in 200 stores initially, and forecast that they would sell 22,000 units per annum. Within 12 months, however, the sales volume had increased to 30,000 units. As a result, the distribution was increased to 560 stores in April 2010 and the Tangle Teezer Magic Flowerpot and Compact Styler were also introduced. The original Tangle Teezer is now forecast to sell more than 50,000 units by April 2011.

IN 2008 *Shaun Pulfrey's Tangle Teezer business (see previous page) had a turnover of £95,991, a gross profit of £31,605, but a net loss before tax of £18,251. As sales increased, turnover went up to £427,204 in 2009; gross profit rose to £288,753 and the net profit before tax became £127,425. These were impressive figures, as they took into account only the first few months of sales through Boots, which has become a big customer for Shaun, as evidenced by the 2010 turnover, which was over £800,000.*

- **INCREASING PRICES.** A £1 increase in the 'top line' goes directly to the 'bottom line' in that it directly increases your profit. Although increasing prices is one of the most effective strategies to increase profits, it is also one of the most difficult and uncompetitive. A better strategy may be to charge different prices to different customer niches as some niches may be less resilient to price increases than others. Another way to justify an increase in prices is by investing in quality.

- **CONTROLLING COSTS.** You may be able to reduce costs by renegotiating prices with suppliers or sourcing lower cost components. You may be able increase productivity to generate more output from the same cost of inputs.

There is an obvious conflict between some of these options. For example discounting to increase sales volume and increasing prices. The most effective combination of techniques will depend on the nature of your business. Changing your product mix from lower- to higher-margin products will also improve gross profit margin.

HOW TO CALCULATE NET PROFIT MARGIN

This is similar to gross margin but takes account of operating expenses (or overheads). Net profit margin measures the ability to control costs.

$$\text{operating (net) profit margin \%} = \frac{\text{operating profit}}{\text{revenue}} \times 100$$

HOW TO INCREASE NET PROFIT MARGIN

The net profit margin is improved by controlling overheads and cutting discretionary costs.

- **CONTROLLING OVERHEADS.** Good methods include investing in efficient administration; more effective staff utilization; optimizing use of power; negotiating cheaper leases/rents; and sourcing cheaper financing.

- **CUTTING DISCRETIONARY COSTS.** Many businesses cut assumed 'discretionary' costs such as travel, entertainment, research and product development costs. With regard to travel, the growth in budget airlines has been fuelled by commercial as well as domestic travellers

– many businesses now view non-economy travel as a discretionary cost. However, whilst discretionary costs may help to improve short-term profit they often have long-term consequences that can have a disproportionate effect on long-term profitability.

"I MADE THE DECISION TO HAVE AN IMPRESSIVE BALANCE SHEET RATHER THAN AN IMPRESSIVE FOYER " DUNCAN BANNATYNE, DRAGON

MAXIMIZING YOUR USE OF INVESTMENT

'Investment' is typically measured as 'capital employed', which is effectively the amount invested in a business by both shareholders and debt holders (equity plus non-current liabilities or, alternatively, total assets less current liabilities).

HOW TO CALCULATE ASSET TURNOVER

This shows how well the finance invested in assets (generally long-term assets, inventory and receivables less payables) has been utilized to generate sales. It measures the amount of revenue earned from each £1 invested.

$$\text{asset turnover (times)} = \frac{\text{revenue}}{\text{capital employed}}$$

Asset turnover demonstrates the number of 'times' assets generate their value, in terms of revenue. It is sometimes referred to as a measure of 'activity' and shows if a business is maximizing the use of its investment. A relatively high asset turnover could indicate efficient use of assets, although the measure is sensitive to the valuation of assets. Consider, for example, a bicycle shop that stocks expensive, top-of-the-range bikes and equipment. The shop doesn't sell many bikes as they are beyond the budget of their customers. The shop therefore experiences low asset turnover.

GROWING YOUR RETURN ON INVESTMENT (ROI)

Return on assets is an important indicator of management performance and financial control. It is also a crucial measure used by investors. (See also Commandment 6 on finding investor finance and Commandment 10 on selling a business.)

HOW TO CALCULATE ROI

$$ROI\% = \text{net profit margin} \times \text{asset turnover}$$

or

$$ROI\% = \frac{\text{operating profit}}{\text{revenue}} \times \frac{\text{revenue}}{\text{capital employed}} \times 100$$

Return on Investment (ROI) is also known as Return on Capital Employed (ROCE). There are other similar measures in practice. Analysing the net profit margin and asset turnover will help to explain a high or low ROCE.

SHOES GALORE

When Shoes Galore first made an appearance on Dragons' Den, the company's owner, Lesley-Ann Simmons, was seeking to expand her franchise business, which sold shoes and accessories using the

ONE OF SHOES GALORE'S *selling points was stocking the same style in many colour variations.*

party plan model. Within less than a year of starting, Lesley-Ann had sold 21 franchises; the business had a healthy turnover and was profitable.

As it was an investment proposal, though, the Dragons scrutinized the business and figures closely to understand what growth would mean for the Shoes Galore franchise. Lesley-Ann was offered salient advice by Theo, after he had questioned her about stock (inventory).

Having ascertained that she had about £65,000 of stock (£25,000 of which was out-of-season stock and £40,000 of which was forward-purchased stock for autumn) and that she proposed using £50,000 of the investment to buy new stock for the following summer to supply an anticipated 50 franchises, Theo warned about the dangers of overtrading. To service further franchises, Lesley-Ann would have to buy increasing quantities of stock, so using up large amounts of cash and creating a larger and larger amount of dead stock, since the business model was not based on having season-end sales.

Lesley-Ann left the Den without investment, but with a useful piece of advice about business growth. Soon after, she decided to sell the Shoes Galore business, still in a healthy state, and sold off the old stock in a clearance sale.

THEO IMPLORED LESLEY-ANN *to think of the money. Because she stocked each style of shoe in a wide range of colours, she needed a high level of stock to provide a decent choice of styles for customers. And large stock levels for an increased number of franchisees would mean a lot of money tied up in a lot of stock sitting on shelves waiting to be sold. Lesley-Ann agreed, and selling the business has given her the time, money and freedom to search for a new business venture for 2010 and beyond.*

CONTROLLING SHORT-TERM SOLVENCY AND LIQUIDITY

Short-term solvency is an essential part of financial control and is the ability to meet short-term debts from liquid assets. Liquid assets refers to your cash and other assets that can be quickly turned into cash, such as money on short-term deposit and trade receivables. Note that although inventories (or stock) are current assets they do not count as liquid assets, as the ability to turn them quickly into cash is debatable.

UNDERSTAND LIQUIDITY VERSUS PROFITABILITY

Whereas profitability is the return generated by a business, liquidity is the ability to pay expenses and debts as and when they fall due.

Liquidity is essential for the financial stability of any business. A failure to manage liquidity may lead to a business being unable to pay its suppliers and debt holders, which may ultimately lead to insolvency.

"TURNOVER IS VANITY, PROFIT IS SANITY, BUT CASH IS REALITY"

Many growing businesses fail from a lack of cash, rather than from a lack of sales.

A useful analogy is that profit is like food, whereas cash is like oxygen. The survival 'rule of threes' states that people can survive three weeks without food, three days without water, but only three minutes without oxygen. Similarly, a business can survive without profit in the short term but it can not survive without cash – put it this way, if you stop paying your employees and suppliers your business will not survive for very long at all.

Although this sounds simple, many growing businesses don't place enough attention on their liquidity. Firstly, businesses aren't realistic when forecasting their cash income and cash expenses. Generally, they overestimate income and underestimate expenses. Secondly, not enough businesses regularly forecast cash flow and foresee problems before they arise. When they run out of cash it's often too late.

Naturally, both a healthy cash flow and high profits are the ideal goals, but in practice they are not that easy. The short-term goal of a business should be to manage cash flow, and the medium- to long-term goal to manage profitability.

A business can have the best service or product in its market, but if it runs out of cash, the quality won't matter. Consider, for example, a premium car retailer selling a low number of high-priced new vehicles and a secondhand car retailer selling many low-priced vehicles. The premium car retailer is likely to have more profits than the secondhand car retailer. However, the secondhand car retailer could easily have more cash than the high-price business and therefore more liquidity and better ability to survive than the premium car retailer.

CONTROLLING THE GROWTH

Many businesses strive for growth. There is a belief that fast growth is the best way to build a successful business. However, rapid growth may not be the best option for businesses with relatively low cash and limited access to new external finance.

SHOES GALORE *(see pp100–1) offered a very good example in the Den of recognizing the dangers of overtrading. The longer the gap between orders, expenditure and income, the greater the danger to the liquidity of a business.*

- **THE OVERTRADING TRAP.** A challenge faced by many growing businesses is the overtrading trap. 'Overtrading' is the imbalance between the work a business receives and its capacity to do it. Overtrading is a symptom of fast-growing businesses, which chase sales and profitability at the expense of liquidity.

  This is common in small growing businesses that offer long credit periods to customers in order to grow market share. At the same time suppliers only offer short credit periods (or insist on cash payments) as small businesses have a limited track record.

This gap between paying suppliers and receiving cash from customers is often financed via overdrafts. Eventually overtraded businesses enter a negative cycle whereby banks will not extend their overdraft any further. Growing interest costs and the associated debt means their financial status eventually reaches insolvency.

- **THE INEFFICIENCIES OF OVERCAPITALIZATION.**
  At the opposite end of the spectrum to overtrading is overcapitalization. An overcapitalized business has excess assets, which are not being utilized effectively. In essence it is not maximizing returns in relation to the size of its assets and in particular its cash. This is not as risky as overtrading but the money should be used to finance long-term projects or returned to shareholders. Overcapitalization is often a symptom of a previously successful, mature business with minimal future growth prospects.

- **FINDING THE BALANCE.** It is difficult for a growing business to turn away sales but success can kill a business as quickly as failure. Controlled and managed growth is critical to the future of a business. Growth demands investment and only a certain level of growth can be financed by internally generated cash. Further growth requires external investment and there's only so much money shareholders will commit and banks will lend in the short term.

MEASURING SHORT-TERM SOLVENCY AND LIQUIDITY

You can measure short-term solvency and liquidity by measuring the current and quick ratios and the cash operating cycle.

HOW TO CALCULATE THE CURRENT RATIO

This is a standard test of short-term solvency and simply measures if a business can meet its current liabilities from its current assets.

$$\text{current ratio} \quad = \quad \frac{\text{current assets}}{\text{current liabilities}}$$

Depending upon the nature of the business, the current ratio should usually be greater than 1, depending upon the speed of inventory turnover.

HOW TO CALCULATE THE QUICK RATIO (OR ACID TEST RATIO)

This is a more reliable short-term solvency measure, as inventory is not easily convertible into cash for many businesses.

$$\text{quick ratio} \quad = \quad \frac{\text{current assets less inventory}}{\text{current liabilities}}$$

This ratio should be close to 1, depending upon the business.

Don't interpret current and quick ratios too literally. Different businesses operate in different ways. Low ratios are not always indicative of insolvency risk and high ratios are not always healthy. For example, a high-volume retailer such as a supermarket could have

" CREDITORS HAVE BETTER MEMORIES THAN DEBTORS; CREDITORS ARE A SUPERSTITIOUS SECT, GREAT OBSERVERS OF SET DAYS AND TIMES "

BENJAMIN FRANKLIN (1706–90), AMERICAN PHILOSOPHER

healthy liquidity but very low current and quick ratios. Supermarkets have relatively low inventories as their goods are mainly perishable and turnover quickly. They have minimal receivables as customers pay in cash. In addition, their purchasing power results in long trade payable payment periods. Therefore overall the supermarkets have relatively low current assets and relatively high current liabilities.

A poorly managed business with slow-selling inventories and many outstanding receivables may have high current and quick ratios. If that's a description of your business, then your short-term solvency and liquidity are at stake and you need to work out where you can improve cash flow in the cash operating cycle.

UNDERSTANDING THE CASH OPERATING CYCLE

The cash operating cycle is the length of time between paying out cash for purchases and receiving cash for sales. It is also referred to as the working capital cycle or cash conversion cycle. It is a useful measure of the time taken to generate cash.

You should understand, measure, control, finance and where possible minimize the length of your cash operating cycle. You will probably also find it useful to find out about the cash operating cycles of your customers, suppliers and competitors.

The cash operating cycle is normally measured in days and is represented by the diagram below, using the example of a manufacturer.

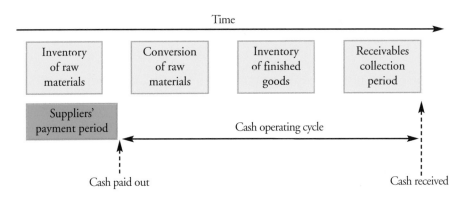

The duration of the cycle and the amount of working capital required is determined by a number of factors, such as the type of industry and the ability of a business to manage the cycle efficiently. Here are examples of the cycle in three different types of businesses:

- **SERVICE BUSINESSES.** A consultancy working on long-term projects may have lots of money owed to them for unbilled work-in-progress as well as long receivable collection periods. Their main input cost will be consultants, who have no payment period. A small consultancy business may have difficulty financing long cash operating cycles. As such, it is common practice for consultancies to ask for stage payments from their clients on a long project.

- **SEASONAL BUSINESSES.** Seasonal businesses, such as calendar and diary manufacturers have fluctuating operating cycles. Production is spread throughout the year and inventories will gradually build up. Trade receivables will increase from a low start as retailers stock up for the peak sales season, but may not pay until after the season. The supplier's payment period will be negligible and therefore seasonal manufacturers will require several months of financing.

- **RETAILERS.** A large retailer such as a supermarket will have a relatively low finished goods inventory period (due to perishables) and minimal receivables as the majority of their sales are in cash. In addition, due to their size and purchasing power they can negotiate extended payment terms with suppliers. Therefore, some supermarkets will actually have a negative cash operating cycle, in that they receive cash from customers before they have to pay suppliers.

" I KEEP TELLING PEOPLE THAT CASH FLOW IS ONE OF THE MOST IMPORTANT THINGS IN BUSINESS. TOO MANY GOOD IDEAS FAIL BECAUSE THEY DON'T HAVE ENOUGH MONEY COMING THROUGH. "

THEO PAPHITIS, DRAGON

HOW TO MEASURE THE CASH OPERATING CYCLE

The chart below shows the cycle for the manufacturer in the diagram on p108. Business growth that will affect the cycle in the future and seasonality that will affect the cycle at different times of the year should also be considered.

$$\text{Raw materials holding period} = \frac{\text{average raw materials inventory}}{\text{annual raw material usage}} \times 365 = X$$

$$\text{Materials conversion period} = \frac{\text{average work in progress inventory}}{\text{annual cost of sales}} \times 365 = X$$

$$\text{Finished goods inventory period} = \frac{\text{average finished goods inventory}}{\text{annual cost of sales}} \times 365 = X$$

$$\text{Receivables collection period} = \frac{\text{average receivables}}{\text{annual sales}} \times 365 = X$$

$$\text{Suppliers' payment period} = \frac{\text{average trade payables}}{\text{annual purchases}} \times 365 = (X)$$

LENGTH OF CYCLE   X

HOW TO CONTROL THE CASH OPERATING CYCLE TO IMPROVE LIQUIDITY

Cash tied up in inventory or money owed by customers cannot be used to pay short-term obligations and therefore you need to try and release cash in the ways described opposite.

- **MINIMIZE INVENTORY LEVELS.** There are many methods of inventory management. A well known technique is JIT ('just-in-time'), used mainly in manufacturing. Goods are produced only to meet customer demand. All inventory arrives from suppliers just-in-time for the next stage in the production process. This technique minimizes inventory levels.

- **MINIMIZE AND CONTROL CASH OWED BY CUSTOMERS.** It is important to follow procedures and be organized in collecting customer debts. The simplest way to avoid having money tied in customer debt is to insist that customers pay in cash. However, to be competitive and attract customers many businesses have no choice but to offer credit. Note too that offering settlement discounts as an incentive for customers to pay on time or early can be expensive. Businesses should ensure the cost of offering a discount does not outweigh the benefits.

- **MAXIMIZE THE PAYMENT PERIOD TO SUPPLIERS.** Delaying payments to suppliers will not generate cash but it will delay its outflow. Many businesses use supplier credit as a source of finance (see Commandment 6 – Finance Your Growth). Extended credit should be negotiated as opposed to taken, to avoid problems in the future. Businesses rely on their suppliers to keep their operations flowing so payment terms should always be agreed in advance.

ADEJARE DOHERTY AND HIS WHOLELEAF COMPANY *featured in Series 7. At the time, the cost of producing their sustainable and ethically produced disposable tableware was equivalent to the price they could sell them into supermarkets – hence no profit margin. Adejare's plan at the time was to get the products made in sufficient numbers to bring the cost down considerably, but the Dragons didn't think he'd sell the numbers he'd need to and so didn't invest. Since then, though, Adejare has been able to negotiate decent credit terms with the company's suppliers, which has offset the amounts of capital tied up in stock (inventory). They are also now working with a number of distributors, including Remmerco and Pronto Pack.*

MANY BUSINESSES WITH CASH DIFFICULTIES DON'T REALIZE THEY ARE IN TROUBLE UNTIL IT'S TOO LATE

USING CASH FLOW FORECASTS

Cash flow forecasts enable businesses to predict and deal with liquidity problems and they are one of the most important measures of future solvency. Here are three ways in which they will help you:

1 **USE THEM WHEN YOU PLAN TO CHANGE THINGS.** A cash flow forecast will demonstrate the sensitivity of cash flow to changes in sales, margins and overheads.

2 **USE THEM TO MINIMIZE THE COST OF CASH SHORTFALLS.** From a cash flow forecast you will see how much money you need to borrow in advance. Banks will generally offer businesses more favourable arrangements for planned as opposed to unplanned overdrafts or loans.

3 **USE THEM TO MAXIMIZE THE BENEFITS OF CASH SURPLUSES.** If you've forecasted surplus cash you can invest it in a short-term deposit account, for example.

A cash flow forecast should be produced regularly and frequently and updated as events unfold. They are most commonly produced monthly and some businesses even produce weekly or daily forecasts.

HOW TO CREATE A CASH FLOW FORECAST

A four-month extract of a simple cash flow forecast is shown in the example below. The aim is to show a net monthly cash flow and the resulting impact on the cash balance. The cash balance should correspond to the business bank account, and usually you would itemize the cash inflows and outflows.

Note in the example below that January, March and April have positive closing cash balances, whereas February is forecasting an overdraft of £2,500.

	January £	February £	March £	April £
Cash inflows	10,000	12,000	15,000	14,000
Cash outflows	(7,000)	(18,500)	(10,500)	(10,000)
Monthly net cash flow	3,000	(6,500)	4,500	4,000
Opening cash balance	1,000	4,000	(2,500)	2,000
Closing cash balance	4,000	(2,500)	2,000	6,000

Be prudent when making a cash flow forecast. Income should be underestimated as customers don't always pay on time, whilst expenses should be overestimated in case of unexpected bills. The cash flow should thus always be a 'worst-case scenario'.

CONTROLLING LONG-TERM SOLVENCY AND STABILITY

Long-term solvency ratios measure the risk faced by a business from its debt burden. Debt interest must be paid irrespective of cash generation or profits. Consequently, the amount of profit that can be reinvested in the business or paid as dividends is diluted. Additionally, an excessive debt burden will restrict the ability of a business to raise further debt finance. (See Commandment 6 for more on debt finance.)

HOW TO CALCULATE THE GEARING RATIO

Gearing (or leverage) is a measure of a business's long-term financing arrangements (or capital structure). It is essentially the proportion of a business financed via debt compared to equity. The higher the gearing, the riskier the business in terms of dilution of earnings and sensitivity to changes in interest rates.

$$\text{gearing ratio \%} = \frac{\text{interest bearing debt - cash}}{\text{equity + (interest bearing debt - cash)}} \times 100$$

The ideal proportion is subject to the nature of a business and the current economic climate. In practice many businesses have gearing levels less than 50%.

" INVESTMENT IS ABOUT PUTTING MONEY IN AND GETTING MORE MONEY OUT. IT'S AMAZING HOW MANY PEOPLE DON'T REALIZE THAT. "

DUNCAN BANNATYNE, DRAGON

HOW TO CALCULATE THE DEBT RATIO

This measures the ability of a business to meet its debts in the long term. It is a measure of 'security' for financiers. The ratio should certainly be less than 100% and many believe it should be less than 50%.

$$\text{debt ratio \%} = \frac{\text{total debts (current and non-current liabilities)}}{\text{total assets (current and non-current assets)}} \times 100$$

The risk posed from high debt and gearing ratios can be mitigated by high interest cover (see below).

HOW TO CALCULATE INTEREST COVER

This measures how many times a business can pay its interest charges (finance expenses) from its operating profit (profit before interest and tax). Ideally a business should be able to cover its interest at least two or more times. The ability to service debt is a measure of risk to debt providers, shareholders and ultimately the business itself.

$$\text{Interest cover (times)} = \frac{\text{operating profit}}{\text{finance expenses}}$$

HOW TO CALCULATE NET DEBT TO EBITDA

EBITDA means 'earnings before interest, tax, depreciation and amortization' and is a popular measure of profit. Cash generated from operations can be substituted for EBITDA. This ratio is often used by investors as a measure of gearing:

$$\text{net debt to EBITDA (times)} = \frac{\text{interest bearing debt - cash}}{\text{EBITDA}}$$

Net debt to EBITDA demonstrates the potential ability of a business to service its debt burden from its earnings, therefore it is used by banks to decide the amount of debt it will provide to a business. Although it depends upon the business and the industry, banks will typically lend a business up to five times its earnings.

USING AN ACCOUNTANT

Many businesses just use their accountant to prepare financial statements for their end-of-year tax return. However, an accountant can provide other value-added services, such as assistance with budgets, preparation and review of financial information and general advice regarding financial control. In addition, you will probably need extra bookkeeping assistance as your business grows.

If your business grows a lot you might want to consider recruiting an in-house accountant to focus on financial strategy leaving you as the entrepreneur to focus on business strategy.

Finally, you should note that if your company grows beyond certain thresholds it will be required to have an external audit performed by accountants.

ISLAND BAKERY ORGANICS

Based on the Isle of Mull, Island Bakery Organics had been producing quality biscuits since 2001. It was run by Joe Reade, and he wanted £150,000 investment to build a new bakery, having reached the limit of production capacity in the company's existing facility.

JOE'S ISLAND LOCATION *on Mull was instrumental to the grant he has obtained.*

On the televised episode, this upscaling seemed to be on a truly massive scale – from 800 sq ft to a whopping 60,000 sq ft – but someone's figures had gone awry at some point during the inquisition and Joe hadn't corrected the error in time. Joe's expansion plans were certainly big, but not megalomaniacal. His old bakery was indeed 800 sq ft but the new bakery was planned to be just 6,000 sq ft, not ten times that figure.

Nevertheless, Duncan had picked up on an important point regarding any business's plans for expansion, which is the attendant increase in overhead costs – business rates, electricity, heating and so on – all elements that need to be carefully costed. In Joe's case, he had looked into this in considerable detail and come up with an interesting proposition. He had determined that his company could be the UK's, if not the world's, first carbon-neutral commercial bakery by using the island's supply of wood chips from managed forests on Mull as fuel for the ovens. Not only would it make ecological and economic sense, but it would give his organic biscuits a special USP.

Joe may not have got investment from the Dragons, but, with the aid of a bank loan and an EU grant, he is pushing ahead with these plans for the

JOE HAD QUITE AN ORDEAL IN THE DEN. *The Dragons ate his biscuits but made no offers of investment.*

new bakery, which will double the hourly output. With added shifts, Joe will be able to multiply output by a factor of six and, within three years, the business is projecting a doubling in turnover.

ISLAND BAKERY ORGANICS' *range of biscuits.*

FINANCE YOUR GROWTH

Where will the extra funds come from?

FINANCING GROWTH is akin to fuelling the engine that drives a business forward. In other words, you can't grow without finding money from somewhere to fund all those extra expenses that come with growth – the extra equipment, resources, inventory and, not least, the probable need to take on more people. Once you've prepared cash flow forecasts for growth (see previous chapter), you should have a clear idea about how much money you need and when. You are then faced with a wide variety of financing options, which we will cover in this chapter to help you identify the best source of funds for your growing business.

INTERNALLY GENERATED FINANCE

Funds that the business has generated itself are obviously the first place you should consider to finance your growth. There are several possible internal sources:

RETAINED PROFITS

As your business grows there will hopefully be excess earnings after expenses to reinvest in further growth. See Commandment 5 for methods of increasing revenues and reducing costs to increase profit. If you have a Limited Company, bear in mind that reinvesting retained profits means there will be less funds available for dividends payments. Shareholders must therefore be willing to sacrifice short-term gains for long-term growth.

WORKING CAPITAL MANAGEMENT

Managing working capital efficiently can release cash to help finance business growth. See p111 for tips on managing liquidity.

SELLING SURPLUS ASSETS

Idle fixed assets, for example unused equipment, and inventory for slower-moving product lines could be sold for cash.

DELAYING THE PURCHASE OF NEW ASSETS

Extending the replacement cycle of existing assets, such as computers or company vehicles, helps to prioritize cash for short-term opportunities. If capital expenditure cannot be delayed, some suppliers may be receptive to renegotiating the price and payment terms.

CLIVE BILLING FAILED TO GET INVESTMENT *for his new 'click-and-buy' diamond web-based business in the Den (see pp64–5). However, the extra revenue he accrued from his existing site (Diamond Geezer) following the Den experience produced enough internally generated funds to launch the new site (Loving the Bead), without him needing to approach any other investors.*

INVESTOR FINANCE

If the business does not have enough funds to finance the growth, then the other major sources are self funding, re-approaching the original investors, supplier and customer finance, private (or angel) investors, venture capitalists, IPOs and DPOs. We will look at each.

INVESTOR FINANCE – SELF FUNDING

Business owners often finance business growth themselves. Typical sources are:

- **SELLING PERSONAL ASSETS.** These might be savings or share portfolios (hopefully for a profit). Some business owners sell off personal collections such as Star Wars memorabilia, old coins and vintage cars to raise money –

SEAN PULFREY OF TANGLE TEEZER *(see p95) re-mortgaged his Brixton flat to finance the product development stage of his new type of hair brush. When it came time to formalize the business, he took out a director's loan of £100,000, which, because of the fast success of the business, he was able to pay back in Year Two.*

many think of it as self-investment as they can always replace these items once they have made lots of money.

- **RE-MORTGAGING.** If you don't happen to have personal assets like those described above but you are a home-owner then you could consider re-mortgaging your property to finance your business growth. However, you should seek independent financial advice before you go down this route.

INVESTOR FINANCE – FUNDS FROM FAMILY AND FRIENDS

Family and friends may be happy to invest in a successful business. However, be aware of the repercussions of relying too much on family and friends who may decide to take an active interest in the business! If any of these people invested in your business when you first launched it, then you should have an idea of how they behave as investors. You could discuss terms such as these:

- **AN INVESTMENT (OR INCREASE IN INVESTMENT) FOR A STAKE (OR BIGGER STAKE) IN THE BUSINESS.** As an example, in the first year of The Body Shop, Anita Roddick sold half of the business to her friend, Ian McGlinn, for a desperately needed $7,000. She had no business experience and could not contact her husband Gordon, who was trekking from Brazil to New York. McGlinn's stake was worth more than $200m when The Body Shop was sold to L'Oréal in 2006!

- **A SHORT-TERM LOAN TO BE REPAID WHEN THE BUSINESS MATURES.** Second time around, many original investors might prefer a loan, especially if you offer a definite repayment deadline.

INVESTOR FINANCE – SUPPLIERS AND CUSTOMERS

Many businesses work successfully with their suppliers and customers to help finance their growth. This does not have to be a formal equity stake – many suppliers and customers are willing to work with growing businesses to develop a relationship that will be beneficial in the future. Examples include:

- Guaranteed demand from customers and marketing support.

THE DRAGONS ARE OFTEN CHARACTERIZED AS BUSINESS ANGELS *as, within the scope of the Dragons' Den programme, that tends to be the kind of investment being pitched to them – early stage businesses and business ideas that they'll speculate on. However, some business opportunities presented to them are more developed and the investment stakes are higher. In these situations, they act more as venture capitalists (see p128), and are thus sometimes described as such.*

- Favourable credit terms from suppliers.
- Purchases on consignment.

INVESTOR FINANCE – PRIVATE (OR ANGEL) INVESTORS

The single largest source of early stage capital comes from private investors. Within the UK alone this is estimated to be between £800 million and £1 billion annually.

Private investors are wealthy individuals who look for businesses with high-growth potential that fill a niche in their portfolios or offer an idea so dazzling that they are willing to take a bet on it. Some such investors may be interested in personally contributing their time to the business, bringing 'added value' through existing business contacts and experience. They tend to be described as 'business angels' when they want to be involved. Indeed, involvement is one of their key benefits, because angel investors bring a wealth of experience of achieving business growth. The Dragons themselves are often described as business angels or angel investors (see left).

Angel investors might invest sums as small as £25,000 or as large as £1 million. They sometimes group together for larger investments. They will usually require a sizeable equity stake and involvement in decision-making. The size of the stake will depend on their required control, valuation of the business, amount of finance needed and good old negotiation.

Angel investors can be found through:

- Word of mouth through **CUSTOMERS, SUPPLIERS, SOLICITORS** or **ACCOUNTANTS**.

- The local **CHAMBERS OF COMMERCE** (www.britishchambers.org.uk/), **BUSINESS LINK** (www.businesslink.gov.uk) or **TRADE ASSOCIATIONS**.

- The **BRITISH BUSINESS ANGELS ASSOCIATION** (www.bbaa.org.uk) is a trade association which encompasses many other networks of private investors.

- The **OXFORD INVESTMENT OPPORTUNITY NETWORK** (OION; www.oion.co.uk) won the 2009 BBAA Award for Business Angel Network of the Year.

Business angels and other private investors can be hard to get access to and difficult to convince. We would recommend that you read *Dragons' Den: The Perfect Pitch* if you are intending to approach any such investors. They require a solid business plan, commitment, tenacity and an exit strategy. Dealing with different private investors can be difficult as each may require different terms. Once you have one or more on board, though, they can lead to significant benefits for the small, growing business.

" IT IS OFTEN PREFERABLE TO HAVE A SMALL SLICE OF A LARGE PIE THAN A LARGE SLICE OF A SMALL PIE " ANON

INVESTOR FINANCE – VENTURE CAPITALISTS (VCs)

Whilst the sort of angel or private investors described above are often involved with young entrepreneurial companies in the early stages of growth, venture capitalist firms (VCs) tend to be interested in the later stages of a growing business and need hurdle rates of at least 25–30% return on investment. VC funding is especially suited to high-growth businesses or ones with viable cutting-edge ideas. VCs often have strict investment criteria such as the stage of the business development, geography, the type of industry or the size of the funding. VCs are usually active in the management of a business and invest sums upwards from £1.5m and typically far higher. They usually exit within five years and often via an IPO (see below).

A listing of VC firms in the UK is at www.financedirector.com. Again, we recommend you read *Dragons' Den: The Perfect Pitch* if you plan to approach any. Indeed, persuading a venture capitalist firm even simply to read through a business plan is tough – they can be very choosy as they receive lots of investment opportunities.

INVESTOR FINANCE – INITIAL PUBLIC OFFERING (IPO)

An Initial Public Offering is the commonly used term for 'floating' a business on a stock exchange and offering shares to the public. This is probably the most expensive way to finance a company. Fees for underwriters, lawyers and investment banks take a sizeable portion of the proceeds (anything between 13–25%). It is a challenging proposition as there is competition for limited funds from the several hundred IPOs launched each year, and the process can take anything from four months to two years. A further consideration is the additional administrative burden and disclosure requirements for public companies. The success of an IPO is not just determined by a business's financial viability. It also hinges on factors such as the state of the economy and overall investor sentiment.

IPOs are not really appropriate for small businesses, but if you are pitching to angel investors or VCs it may be useful for you to offer the future prospect of an IPO as an exit strategy.

INVESTOR FINANCE – DIRECT PUBLIC OFFERING (DPO)

A Direct Public Offering (DPO) can be a more cost-effective method of attracting equity investors for smaller businesses. Depending upon local regulations they can be exempt from many of the reporting and administration requirements needed for an IPO.

A DPO works well for a business with intensely loyal customers who are keen for the business to succeed for their own benefit. They are fairly popular in the US to raise funds ranging from below $1 million up to about $5 million.

EXAMPLES OF COMPANIES USING DPOS

- In 1984, to raise funds for a new manufacturing facility, Ben and Jerry's sought their first outside investment via a direct public offering open only to residents of Vermont.

- In 1995, to raise funds for expanding distribution, Hahnemann Laboratories (a Californian manufacturer of homeopathic medicines) approached its 2,000 customers and managed to raise $470,000 from 240 investors.

- In the mid-1990s, when its revenue was just $6 million, Williamette Valley Vineyards (one of the largest boutique wineries in Oregon, US), raised $5.3 million from four DPOs. The company now has revenues of $16 million and is listed on the NASDAQ stock exchange.

In the UK, the closest equivalent to a DPO is a listing on **PLUS** (www.plusmarketsgroup.com) or **AIM** (Alternative Investment Market – see listing on www.londonstockexchange.com). These are both small and mid-cap stock exchanges with lower fees and more straightforward listing processes than the main market.

THE DRAGONS OFTEN ASK ENTREPRENEURS *why they don't just go to a bank for a loan. Anthony Coates-Smith and Alistair Turner of Igloo Thermo-logistics (Series 4) turned the argument around to use as leverage in negotiations with the Dragons. When Duncan Bannatyne offered them the £160,000 they were after for 40% equity (they came offering only 8%) they recountered that they could achieve the investment at a lower cost to them by going to the bank for a loan. The argument worked and they eventually agreed a joint offer from Duncan and former Dragon Richard Farleigh for a 22.5% stake.*

DEBT FINANCING

This type of financing covers bank loans, overdrafts, asset-based lending and finance leases, which we'll look at in turn.

DEBT FINANCING – BANK LOANS

Bank loans are reliable, tried and tested and can be the cheapest form of financing. They don't dilute shareholder's equity and the fees for processing are usually nominal. Many large banks have departments exclusively focused on lending to small growing businesses. The interest rate on a bank loan will depend upon a business's perceived credit-worthiness – once a good payment record has been established it may be possible to negotiate a lower rate. Unfortunately, the global

WHEN SAMMY FRENCH'S COMPANY FIT FOR LIFE *(see pp138–9) needed a cash injection, the simplest way to obtain the funds would have been to get a bank loan. Indeed, Sammy had pursued this approach. However, this was at the start of the UK's economic downturn, and, without a property to use as a guarantee for the loan, the bank ultimately decided not to issue the money. It was then that she decided to release equity in the business as a way to gain investment. By obtaining that investment from a Dragon, she also got the benefit of some terrific strategic advice on how to push her business forward.*

financial crisis which commenced in the late 2000s led to a restriction of bank finance. When banks find it difficult to raise finance on the wholesale credit markets, they are less willing to loan finance to businesses without an impeccable credit rating.

Bank loans are often secured on assets, such as inventory, equipment or property and many loans have associated covenants which may restrict further borrowing and sale of assets. This is often a challenge for small growing businesses. If a business does not have the required collateral, the banks may demand a personal guarantee.

In the UK, the **ENTERPRISE FINANCE GUARANTEE** scheme aims to help small growing businesses who find it difficult to secure bank finance. The scheme facilitates loans between £1,000 and £1 million and offers to bear 75% of the risk of default of each loan, for a small fee payable by the borrower. Business Link provides information about the scheme (www.businesslink.gov.uk).

A good strategy can be to maintain a 'portfolio' of bank finance with different maturities to match the life of different assets and financing requirements. For example, a long-term loan for fixed assets such as equipment, a medium-term loan (12–18 months) for inventory purchases and to fund accounts receivable, and an overdraft (see below) for fluctuating working capital or cash flow requirements.

DEBT FINANCING – OVERDRAFTS

Overdrafts are one of the most common sources of finance for small businesses. Their key advantage (compared to a bank loan) is their flexibility because the business only uses and pays interest on what they need. Business overdrafts are widely available and collateral is usually not required, although a personal guarantee is often required, especially for new businesses. The key disadvantages are that the interest rate on overdrafts tends to be higher than that for loans and they are technically repayable on demand.

Many businesses negotiate a 'committed facility' each year with their bank. This provides some assurance that the bank will 'honour' the overdraft for the following 12 months. In return the bank will require a sound business plan.

For medium- to long-term finance a loan is cheaper and more suitable than an overdraft.

DEBT FINANCING – ASSET-BASED LENDING

Asset-based lending (or 'factoring') arrangements are revolving loans from commercial banks or commercial finance firms, secured on assets such as property, equipment, stock, accounts receivable and even intellectual property. The size of the loan can be as low as £10,000 or as high as £500,000.

Asset-based lending is popular with small growing businesses and a useful method of financing cash flow shortages. However, businesses can become reliant upon this form of financing, and it is generally more expensive than a bank loan. Therefore, an exit strategy is advised.

Receivables (or debt) factoring is where a business effectively 'sells' their invoices to an asset-based lender, which advances a percentage (typically 85–90%) of the value of either a specific invoice or the whole receivables' (debtors') balance, in advance of collection. There are various types of factoring arrangements ranging from a loan advance to outsourcing debt collection.

Statistics from the **ASSET BASED FINANCE ASSOCIATION**, (www.abfa.org.uk) show that £14bn had been extended in asset lending to 47,000 businesses in the UK and Ireland at the end of 2009 against assets worth £29 billion.

DEBT FINANCING – FINANCE LEASES

Finance leases (or hire purchase) are a useful method of financing assets for growing businesses. At the end of the lease term, the business can renew the lease, return the asset or, with some arrangements, keep the asset for a nominal payment. Small leases (under £30,000) generally require little more than a credit check. Accessing lease finance is often easier, although more expensive than, obtaining bank finance. Soft costs such as installation, costs of maintenance and training, software upgrades and technical support can often be included within the lease financing arrangement.

'Sale and leaseback', commonly used in property transactions, is an increasingly popular form of leasing. A business sells commercial property and leases it back, releasing cash for use in other areas. This can unlock the value 'tied up' within business property. This type of arrangement is possible with other assets such as IT.

Also see below in alternative finance for operating leases.

ALTERNATIVE FINANCE

Other forms of finance for growing businesses include operating leases, credit unions, peer-to-peer lending, grants, sponsorship and strategic opportunities.

OPERATING LEASES

Operating leases are a useful form of financing for growing businesses and are available for copiers, printers, IT equipment and even furniture. No capital outlay or additional security is required, maintenance is often included and the asset can be returned at the end of the lease, avoiding the risk of obsolescence. For small companies the operating lease may not have to be disclosed as a liability on the balance sheet. Bear in mind, however, that the cost of a loan to finance the purchase of the asset may be cheaper than the operating lease.

CREDIT UNIONS

A credit union is a financial co-operative owned and controlled by its members. As well as holding savings they offer loans to members. They are locally based and are open to local individuals as well as local businesses. Interest rates can be lower than high street banks although the amounts available for borrowing are usually much lower. For local businesses credit unions may offer more personal relationships than high street banks.

There are a number of trade associations which represent credit unions such as the **ASSOCIATION OF BRITISH CREDIT UNIONS** (www.abcul.coop), **ACE CREDIT UNION SERVICES** (www.acecus.org) and **UK CREDIT UNIONS** (www.ukcu.co.uk).

PEER-TO-PEER LENDING

Online communities such as Zopa offer peer-to-peer lending (also known as social lending). Borrowers post a loan listing and a number of members offer bids to provide the funding via an online marketplace. The online marketplace connects buyers and sellers and calculates a mutual interest rate and loan term. The principle of supporting a growing business appeals to many community members. Amounts borrowed range from £1,000 to £15,000 and the terms range from one to five years.

Peer-to-peer lending is useful for financing working capital or purchasing assets such as inventory and equipment.

GRANTS

There are many government grants available to help growing businesses that benefit the public or community. For example, the

ENTERPRISE INVESTMENT SCHEME and the **VENTURE CAPITAL TRUST** are government-backed schemes offering tax breaks to investors in small UK businesses. **REGIONAL DEVELOPMENT AGENCIES** (www.englandsrdas.com) and local branches of **BUSINESS LINK** (www.businesslink.gov.uk) can also assist in sourcing public funding.

Pinpointing the right grant can be tedious; the application process is slow; the criteria against which they are awarded are stringent; and once awarded there may be onerous administration requirements. On top of that there is also lots of competition for limited funds from other businesses.

A professional grant writer can help navigate through various different requirements and specifications. A professional tax advisor should be aware of any tax relief schemes which may save money or aid cash flow.

SPONSORSHIP

Large businesses may be willing to sponsor smaller growing businesses in return for positive publicity of their own brand; the ability to reach a specific target market; or other marketing reasons.

For example, a preschool club for young children could seek sponsorship from a designer and developer of children's educational toys, or a business that makes innovative clothes dryers could seek sponsorship from a washing powder brand.

STRATEGIC OPPORTUNITIES

Strategic opportunities such as joint ventures, franchising and licensing can provide alternative methods of raising finance through business partners. See Commandment 10 for more information.

FIT FUR LIFE

Sammy French had started a business selling specialized treadmills for dogs in 2004, two years after coming up with the idea. At the time of visiting the Den in December 2007, however, she had hit a crunch.

SAMMY *developed the idea for a dog treadmill while she was recuperating and needing to use a treadmill herself.*

Sammy had sold 147 units of the first version of the treadmill, but she wanted to develop a better version. She used the profits generated from the sales to develop the Mark II treadmill. However, the development phase consumed all of the profits, and so, when Sammy came to launch the new model at Crufts in 2007, she had the prototype but no actual units to sell. She took orders for 24 machines and then needed a cash injection to pay for an initial production run of 150 units. The profits from the sale of these would then set the company running profitably, and by selling a target of 300 units per year, Sammy's company, Fit Fur Life, would generate a turnover of £480,000. This was the point at which Sammy went into the Dragons' Den. While the future may have looked bright, she was then in a dire financial situation. She had taken deposits for the 24 Mark II treadmills and used part of the money to pay for the tooling of the new machines in the Far East. But without further funds, Sammy wouldn't have been able to pay for the production and shipping of them and her business would have folded. It was a make or break situation.

While some of the Dragons struggled with the concept of a dog treadmill – and the fact that people would pay £1,600 to have one – all thought that Sammy's financial predicament was a problem. However, James Caan saw this as a problem that needed addressing rather than a reason not to invest, and, as he said, Sammy had proved that there was a market for the product. On that basis, he invested in Fit Fur Life. Since then, the business has had a chance to restart.

SAMMY TOOK DELIVERY *of the first consignment of Mark II treadmills in January 2008, and the business has grown rapidly since. Fit Fur Life now sells hundreds of units per quarter and distributes the machines all over the world.*

RECRUIT TALENTED PEOPLE

Do you know how to attract the best?

YOUR BUSINESS IS GROWING, SO YOU NEED MORE PEOPLE. Indeed, maybe up to now your business has had only one full-time employee – you. You probably already know that taking on extra staff means extra responsibilities and obligations, and that a business like yours can't carry dead wood. So first you have to do the groundwork. Make sure you know exactly who you want and why. That's why we're going to spend time on job specifications and deal breakers. No decent recruiter interviews without their deal breakers to hand. This chapter gives you the answers to all your recruitment questions and makes sure the people you want – want you.

WHAT TYPE OF WORKERS DO YOU NEED?

First off, you need to decide what employment terms are best suited to your growing business. Permanent employees, whether full time or part time, present you with the greatest level of responsibilities as an employer (see below), but may be best for certain ongoing roles, e.g. a receptionist. Workers on fixed-term contracts may be best for projects of a fixed duration. Freelancers may be best for sporadic work. Casual or agency staff may be best for seasonal work.

Don't overlook the possibility of using outside contractors for parts of your workflow. For example, marketing can be handled by a marketing company away from your premises (see the example of Youdoo opposite). But always weigh up the pros and cons of in-house staff versus outsourcers. For example, is your volume of orders now so great that it would be cheaper for you to hire full-time drivers rather than use courier companies?

RECRUITMENT AND THE LAW

Let's not pull any punches: if you step outside the law when recruiting then you might be faced with some very expensive consequences. So let's make it easy. If you are considering employing staff on a permanent basis or fixed-term contract then you have to comply with all their rights such as for holidays, sickness, maternity, redundancy and pension, all of which need to be spelled out in a written contract of employment. You are also obliged to pay employers' national insurance and take out employers' liability insurance when you take on permanent or fixed-term workers.

The responsibilities mentioned above are not necessary for freelance or temporary workers. However, whatever terms of

YOUDOO'S SARAH LU *(see pp184–5) started her personalized doll enterprise in a two-bed flat in Brighton. She enlisted friends and family to help stuff dolls, pack products and in some cases deliver stock. As the business has grown, and with Deborah Meaden's investment and advice, Sarah has recruited external people to handle specific parts of the enterprise. Packing and sending out stock has been outsourced to Netlynk Direct in Birmingham, for example, and while Sarah handles UK sales and distribution, a company called Noted in the US handles marketing, sales and distribution in the States. Sarah still carries out a lot of diverse tasks herself – including product design and development, UK sales and distribution, and also PR, marketing and accounts – but she does have a team to run the Youdoo websites.*

employment you are offering, you must comply with basic health and safety requirements. The first book in this series, *Dragons' Den: Start Your Own Business*, has more information about the different forms of insurance and health and safety obligations.

Also, regardless of the form of employment you are offering, bear in mind that from initial advert to choosing the candidate, the following factors shouldn't form any part of your recruitment process: age, disability, gender reassignment, marriage and civil partnership, pregnancy and maternity, race, religion or belief, sex or sexual orientation.

The most obvious and potentially costly pitfall can be unlawful discrimination. There's no limit on compensation and the potential to be sued even starts before employment commences with the advertising stage. So make sure you thoroughly vet your adverts, application forms and CV screening process, interview questions, recording of your decisions, offer letter and employment contracts. And be certain that any other legal documentation is also considered. For example, check if you need to take copies of any passports or visa copies to comply with legislation dealing with illegal working.

For more information on employers' responsibilities see www.businesslink.gov.uk.

WHY FINDING A CLONE OF YOU IS NOT THE ANSWER

Recruitment is one of the trickiest areas for any business, and that's not just because of the legal requirements outlined above. Owners of small, growing businesses especially may be new to recruitment and not really clear about what type of skills they need from workers.

What does the hypothetical perfect worker for your business look like? Don't look in the mirror when you answer this question! Recruiting a clone of you might sound like a smart move but why duplicate skills already in your business? Isn't it better to go out there and think about skills that are different to yours? Your business has a square-shaped hole that someone has to fill. Now you need to set about finding that square-shaped person.

When a football manager has an outstanding target man, they don't busy themselves looking for another target man. They find someone who can feed off them, so they operate as a pair with complementing skills. Think Rush and Dalglish. Think Henry and Bergkamp.

Business is no different. So ask yourself the following:

- What are the skills I bring to the business?
- Which areas am I not strong in?
- What skills will the business need for the future?
- Which areas of the business don't I enjoy?

By now you should see that there are gaps a new person or people could fill. Would you rather saw off your own arm than complete another VAT return? You need to find someone who falls asleep at night reading *'Prime Numbers are My Kind of Fun'*.

" IF EVERYONE IS THINKING ALIKE, THEN SOMEBODY ISN'T THINKING "

GEORGE S. PATTON (1885–1945), US GENERAL OF WORLD WAR II

JOB SPECIFICATIONS

Employers habitually used to have job descriptions and person specifications as two separate documents but many now prefer to wrap them up into one and will give it a title like *'Job Specification'*.

Job specifications are good for several reasons. They help you clearly define the activities and accountabilities of the role, and the typical skills and abilities that candidates need. They help candidates decide whether they should apply for the job or not (known as 'self-screening'). They also demonstrate to candidates that you run your business professionally.

THINGS TO INCLUDE IN A JOB SPECIFICATION

- **JOB TITLE.** An accurate name for the position you're advertising for.

- **JOB PURPOSE AND KEY ACTIVITIES.** A brief overview clarifying why the job exists and what the major responsibilities are.

- **KEY TASKS.** The main duties that the candidate will be expected to undertake.

- **EDUCATION, QUALIFICATIONS AND TRAINING.** The minimum qualifications you expect the candidate to have (be careful – you don't want to 'oversell' the role by putting off good candidates who can't meet the qualifications).

- **EXPERIENCE.** The background and experience you'd expect the candidate to bring with them.

- **KNOWLEDGE.** Specific knowledge that is important to the role (e.g. 'Must have worked with animals before').

- **PERSONAL SKILLS.** These could be behavioural (e.g. dealing with demanding customers) as well as task-based (can manipulate data in a spreadsheet).

- **SPECIAL DEMANDS OF THE ROLE.** Perhaps the candidate will have to work abroad or irregular hours.

Sounds like a bureaucratic nicety? Many would disagree. The moment you bring people in they need to have a clear role with well-defined responsibilities and tasks. That way they know what they need to be concentrating on and can clearly see the boundaries of their job. New people like this!

" THE EMPLOYER GENERALLY GETS THE EMPLOYEES HE DESERVES "

J. PAUL GETTY (1892–1976), AMERICAN INDUSTRIALIST

WHERE TO START LOOKING FOR PEOPLE

Now you know what you want, where do you find it? Of course you might be able to recruit through your network. But isn't it better to give yourself some choice?

PLACING AN ADVERTISEMENT

Advertising is the method favoured by many employers and useful if you're trying to reach a particular audience. Before you place the ad decide who you want to read it and how long it's going to run. You'll want the best return on your money. Don't forget the internet, which is often cheaper than advertising in printed publications, and which allows you to target your audience by locality or sector.

TRUNKI *(see pp48–9) is a company specializing in children's travel products. The owner, Rob Law, describes how he went about finding a key employee: "As a product designer, I couldn't wait to develop more really useful travel products, but I kept finding that my time was taken up with the day-to-day running of the business. After about 18 months of trading, it was time to get some design help and so I went along to a graduate design exhibition in London called New Designers (a show I had exhibited at seven years earlier). It was here I found my Chief Imagineer, Joe. He took over a lot of the design work."*

What about writing the ad itself? A good ad usually contains:

- **COMPANY NAME AND NATURE OF BUSINESS**
- **JOB TITLE**
- **WHERE THE JOB WILL BE LOCATED**
- **KEY DUTIES**
- **QUALIFICATIONS, EXPERIENCE, SKILLS AND KNOWLEDGE NEEDED BY CANDIDATES**
- **SALARY**
- **HOW TO APPLY FOR THE ROLE**
- **CLOSING DATE FOR APPLICATIONS**

The ad is going to need to be concise and interesting – but don't pretend the job is something it's not. Your time is valuable so you won't want to be interviewing candidates who are there only because you 'sexed up' the role.

EMPLOYMENT AGENCIES

Employment agencies can save you a lot of time. Some businesses use them as a source of temporary staff and then convert people they like to permanent status. They're also great for volume recruitment or finding specific skill sets. There are a lot of advantages should you find the right one for your business. The main disadvantage is usually cost – be clear about what the charges will be if you use an agency.

Jobcentre Plus will provide the same services as an employment agency but at no direct cost to your business. You have to register to be an approved employer and list your vacancies – for more details see www.businesslink.gov.uk.

OTHER RECRUITMENT SOURCES

Placing ads and using employment agencies are the most popular ways that people bring in new talent to their business. But there are other sources that you might consider:

- **RECRUITMENT CONSULTANTS AND HEADHUNTERS**
- **ONLINE JOBS FORUMS, E.G. MONSTER.COM**
- **UNIVERSITIES, COLLEGES AND SCHOOLS**
- **TRADE EVENTS** (see the Trunki example opposite)
- **LOCAL ADVERTISING, E.G. POST OFFICES, NEWSAGENTS**

- LOCAL RADIO
- LOCAL AUTHORITY TRAINING SCHEMES
- INTERNAL NOTICEBOARDS
- WORD OF MOUTH / NETWORKING

" THE ABILITY AND CONFIDENCE TO EMPLOY PEOPLE AS GOOD, IF NOT BETTER, THAN ONESELF IS WHAT DRIVES SUCCESS "
JAMES CAAN, DRAGON

HOW TO READ A CV

Great! Your ad's running and you have lots of promising CVs dropping through your post box. But how much can you trust a CV? What do you look for?

- **CONTENT.** Has the applicant crammed in everything including their 100 metre breaststroke badge? Does the content tell you what you need to know?

- **GRAMMAR AND SPELLING.** Is the CV riddled with typos and errors? What does the CV tell you about the candidate's attention to detail?

- **LAYOUT AND DESIGN.** Is it cluttered? How well has it been laid out?

- **JOB HISTORY.** Does their career make sense? Have they a tendency to 'job hop'? Are large periods of time unaccounted for?

- **ACHIEVEMENTS.** Do they list what they've achieved or just duties?

- **CREDIBILITY.** Does it 'feel right'? Are there sudden leaps in status which are at odds with the previous role they had? Are they 'gilding the lily' with their achievements?

Place the job spec on your table and put the CVs in front of you. Now – when you go through each CV – compare their skills and experience with your job spec. Do they match?

Make three CV piles: 'Yes', 'No' and 'Look again'. Stay objective: only reject candidates whose skills and experience do not match your job specification.

A little tip: don't do a big pile of CVs at once because after a while you stop taking in all the information. Break up the task and do a few at a time.

THINK UP QUESTIONS FOR INTERVIEWEES

We prepare questions for interviewees for two reasons:

1 We give each candidate a fair opportunity by asking each the same questions to prove to us they have the right skills for the job.

" START WITH GOOD PEOPLE, LAY OUT THE RULES, COMMUNICATE WITH YOUR EMPLOYEES, MOTIVATE THEM AND REWARD THEM. IF YOU DO ALL THOSE THINGS EFFECTIVELY, YOU CAN'T MISS. "

LEE IACOCCA, PRESIDENT OF THE CHRYSLER CORPORATION

2 We stay focused on objectively assessing a person: recruiting is a hard-headed business.

So how do you write really good interview questions? First decide on five or six 'deal breakers' for the role. A deal breaker is a skill that is a 'must have'. Will your people have to deal with difficult customers? If yes then a friendly but assertive manner will certainly be a deal breaker.

Write a question that asks the candidate to show you where they've demonstrated this deal breaker in the past. Begin your questions with "Tell me about a time…" or "Give me an example of the most difficult customer you've encountered? What happened?"

Why ask for examples? Because the role needs an experienced person. With examples the interviewer will soon be able to assess how much experience they're going to bring. Asking a question like "How would you deal with a difficult customer?" is fine, but it doesn't mean they can do it!

Ask questions that challenge candidates to prove they have the experience you need. Who would you want in your team: someone who's actually calmed down an angry person and got them to be reasonable again, or someone who can theorize about it?

Once you've got a list of 8 – 10 questions you're ready to go. But let's just get you thinking about one more thing...

PROBING THE CANDIDATE

Asking the question is just the beginning. You need to follow up each question with a probe, something that explores the candidate's answer and searches for why they took the action they did. What did they learn? What was their motivation for the action? Would they change their approach now?

So be prepared to take your time and probe that bit deeper. There's a lot riding on this decision so you don't want to rush into it.

TELEPHONE INTERVIEWING

You're sitting with a candidate and are just five minutes into the interview. Already they've fluffed two important questions and you're fast realizing their CV is a serious contender for the Pulitzer Prize for Fiction... Want to find a way of never being in this predicament? Let's talk about telephone interviewing.

Telephone interviewing is a cost effective way of conducting the first 'sift' of candidates. They are relatively short, convenient for both parties and allow you to filter out unsuitable candidates over the phone rather than with an hour-long interview.

Make the call relatively brief, limiting it to the most important facts you want to reassure yourself about. Ask them to talk through their CV and probe on the experience they've cited. Take a 'deal breaker' and try and explore how much real experience they've had.

There are some rules when conducting a telephone interview:

- **TREAT IT LIKE A FACE-TO-FACE INTERVIEW.** Prepare, read the CV and have the same questions that you will ask every candidate.

- **BE PUNCTUAL WHEN YOU CALL.** Impress them with your professionalism from the start.

- **BEGIN WITH A SHORT AGENDA.** How long the interview will last, what general areas you'd like to explore and when they can ask you questions.

- **START WITH EASIER QUESTIONS.** Let the candidate relax. If you discuss their CV use this as an opportunity to build rapport.

- **KEEP TO YOUR FORMAT / STRUCTURE.** Keep the call friendly – but focused.

- **PROBE FOR MORE INFORMATION.** Say things like "I'm particularly interested in that. Could you tell me a bit more?"

- **TELL THE CANDIDATE WHAT THE NEXT STAGE WILL BE.** How are you going to inform them whether they've been successful or not?

GOLDGENIE

When you've been the sole driving force behind the launch of a business, it can be hard to recruit and delegate. It can also be difficult to work out where the business is best served by you personally and what aspects can be left to others.

LABAN ROOMES, *the man behind Goldgenie.*

Even after getting investment in the Den from James Caan, Laban Roomes of Goldgenie was still reluctant to let go of the day-to-day work.

"The first thing James instilled into my head was not to do any more gold plating. He encouraged me to change my role and spend time in meetings and closing deals, as I naturally like meeting people and am very passionate about my products. Before Dragons' Den I did a lot of gold plating myself, but I've learnt that it is better to earn a percentage of other people's efforts than 100% of my own!"

Now employing gold platers, as well as accounts and admin people and a PA, Laban is free to concentrate on developing the business with new marketing ideas, such as the celebrity-endorsed range, 'Bling with Benefits', which gives a percentage of sales to charity.

One last point: don't forget that in the UK a telephone interview falls under the same laws that cover face-to-face interviews.

HOW TO MAKE PEOPLE WANT TO JOIN YOUR COMPANY

You mustn't forget that your candidate is interviewing your company as well. You want a good candidate to say 'yes' to your job offer. So you've got to make them welcome – and make them want to join!

Here are some tips to make them want to be part of your business:

- **WELCOME THEM.** If you have a receptionist let them know the names of who you'll be interviewing – give them a drink when they arrive.

- **PREPARE WELL.** Have your paperwork ready and think about how you'll open the interview.

- **LOOK THE PART.** Show them through your dress and manner that the interview is a serious matter.

- **COLLECT THE CANDIDATE YOURSELF.** If you're the head honcho who will be making the decision, then you should collect them. It lets them know egos aren't welcome.

- **PREPARE AN INTERVIEW ROOM.** You don't want to be disturbed. Arrange the seats in a friendly way preferably around a small circular table.

- **DON'T BORE THEM!** Briefly tell them what the business does and how it does it. Then get on to finding out more about them.

- **SETTLE NERVOUS CANDIDATES.** Try some early rapport building. Your job is to relax them: relaxed candidates will tell you much more.

- **TREAT EVERYONE WITH DIGNITY.** Even if you know early on they're not suitable, manage the situation carefully. Word of mouth is very strong in job hunting.

- **ESCORT THEM WHEN THEY LEAVE THE PREMISES.** You may well get some useful additional information as you walk them back.

WHERE INTERVIEWERS GO WRONG

Think back to your early career. Ever had the experience of being interviewed by someone who hasn't a clue? Here are seven of the deadliest sins…

1 **YOU'RE NOT PREPARED.** Being unprepared for such an important event sends all the wrong signals.

2 **YOU START THE INTERVIEW LATE.** What does this say to the candidate? Be honest: how do you feel when you're kept waiting?

3 **YOU TALK MORE THAN THE CANDIDATE DOES.** You go on and on about the company, your career…

4 **YOU ONLY ASK CLOSED QUESTIONS.** Don't ask "Have you had much experience of selling over the phone?" Ask "What experience have you had of selling over the phone?"

5 **YOU DON'T ASK THE SAME QUESTIONS.** You will have a framework of the same questions you'll ask of each candidate. Of course, your probing questions will depend on the response of the candidate and do no have to be the same.

6 **YOU GO ON 'GUT INSTINCT'.** It sounds very dynamic to say "I know 'em when I see 'em" but we often don't. Your gut instinct may tell you that you like someone – but it doesn't mean they can do the job.

7 **YOU MAKE YOUR MIND UP TOO EARLY.** You leap to a decision about someone and then skew the rest of the interview looking for evidence that confirms your view.

DEALING WITH THEIR QUESTIONS

If they're good then they're going to have some pertinent questions. But be careful – don't get drawn in to questions that you really shouldn't answer. For example, if a candidate asks "Have I got the job?" then be very careful. Become a politician and sidestep the

YOUR GUT INSTINCT MAY TELL YOU THAT YOU LIKE SOMEONE – BUT IT DOESN'T MEAN THEY CAN DO THE JOB

question: "Well, we have several candidates to see and we'll be letting people know our decision very soon."

Be helpful in giving answers but don't talk too much. Remember to talk about the 'successful candidate' when describing duties in the role. If you say "You would be working on end-of-month figures…" then that sounds like a job offer!

MAKING YOUR CHOICE

Once the interviews are finished it's time to make your choice. A good way to help you do this – before you even see the first candidate – is by drawing up an assessment grid. Down one side of the grid put all of the deal breakers that you said were vital. Across the top write the name of each candidate. After each interview go down the deal breakers for the candidate and rate how much they demonstrated evidence of each. Use a scale like:

0 – No evidence of ability in this area
1 – Some evidence of ability; will need development
2 – Has the level of ability required for the role
3 – Exceeds the level of ability required

" THE MAGIC FORMULA THAT SUCCESSFUL BUSINESSES HAVE DISCOVERED IS TO TREAT CUSTOMERS LIKE GUESTS AND EMPLOYEES LIKE PEOPLE "

TOM PETERS, BUSINESS MANAGEMENT WRITER

Now mark each candidate based on your notes from the interview. This grid will help you make an objective decision and keep you focused on the skills you require. Record your decision and reasons for acceptance or rejection of each candidate on each set of interview notes. Before you make your final decision, check up on the references, qualifications and other factual points in the CV.

Make sure you keep the paperwork for all the candidates. In the UK all candidates have a legal right to see what you've written about them. Keep this in mind and store everything for at least one year.

MAKING A JOB OFFER

When you come to make the job offer, make sure you get their acceptance before you inform the unsuccessful candidates. In the UK a verbal offer is as binding as a written offer, so if you're going to phone them with the happy news prepare thoroughly what you're going to say and what you'll be offering. Then follow up with a written offer to them as soon as possible.

DEALING WITH REJECTED CANDIDATES

It's easy to forget the unlucky ones once you've found the one you're looking for. But make sure you send your rejected candidates a letter or email as quickly as possible. Use phrases like "…Unfortunately, on this occasion, your application has not been successful." After all, if the new person you appointed doesn't work out, you may well have a good person from the rejected list waiting to take their place.

Some candidates will ask for feedback as to why they didn't get the job. Many organizations will not give feedback. However, if you want to give feedback, use the telephone – don't email it to them or send it in writing. Make sure the feedback is constructive and let them know which areas of experience you felt they did not communicate enough evidence of.

DRAWING UP A CONTRACT OF EMPLOYMENT

As soon as an applicant unconditionally accepts your job offer, a contract of employment comes into play, even if it is not formally written down. You don't have to write a contract for independent contractors, freelancers and agency workers. However, you are obliged by law to provide permanent or fixed-term employees with some form of written statement of their employment within two months of them starting. In the terms and conditions you should include pay, expected working hours and holiday entitlement. You can also include statements about your employer's duty of care and the employee's duty of honesty and loyal service.

Note that even if you do not mention issues such as sick pay, maternity terms and redundancy in the contract you are still obliged to adhere to the statutory standards. See www.businesslink.gov.uk for example contracts of employment.

You can wrap up the contract of employment together with working practices and policies in an Employee Handbook (see p201).

BECOME A GREAT LEADER

Can you lead your team to success?

ONCE YOU'VE GOT SOME TALENTED PEOPLE on board your growing business, you're going to have to build them up as a team and be their leader. This means letting go of parts of your current job in a way that you might not have anticipated. The opposite of leadership is micromanagement, which is often disastrous in a small business. We'll look at what micromanagers do and why it achieves the wrong results. We'll also see why you must constantly adapt your leadership style to the situations you are likely to find yourself in with a growing business. Respect isn't a given in business – it has to be earned.

WHY DO LEADERS HAVE TO LEARN TO LET GO?

Think back to bosses you've had. If you were lucky, then you've had some great role models who have helped shape your own leadership style. But amongst all the bosses you may have had, who would you prefer to forget? Remember the managers who would not let you get on with it? They'd delegate work to you and then, half an hour later, be looking over your shoulder making sure you're doing it right. The micromanagers whose every action was telling you, "I want to pretend that I trust you but, as you can see, I'm afraid I don't."

So what does micromanaging do? It creates two negative effects:

- **MICROMANAGING STOPS PEOPLE TAKING ANY INITIATIVE.** There's a wonderful saying: "With every pair of hands you get a free brain." If you constantly tell people what to do, then they eventually do nothing until you give them the 'go-ahead'.

- **YOU SEND A MESSAGE THAT EMPLOYEES CAN'T BE TRUSTED.** Ask yourself: how much satisfaction are you going to get when you feel you can't be trusted?

WORKING ON THE BUSINESS – NOT IN THE BUSINESS

If you're really serious about growing your business then you've got to create space to allow this to happen. That means that you have to begin to pass over duties that you used to do. For many entrepreneurs, this is really tough. When you've built up the business from nothing it's hard to pass parts of it over to other people.

" BEING A CEO IS NOT JUST ABOUT YOU. IT COMES DOWN TO YOUR ABILITY TO ATTRACT A TEAM. IT IS TEAMS THAT BUILD AND RUN BUSINESSES. WITHOUT YOU HAVING REAL LEADERSHIP SKILLS, THESE PEOPLE WILL NOT COME. "

JAMES CAAN, DRAGON

But you now have to stop looking down at the business and look up to the horizon. Where's the business going? What are the opportunities you need to be readying yourself for? Where are the pitfalls you're going to have to overcome?

In short: you have to stop managing the business and start leading it. You need to move away from maintenance tasks to those that build your business.

Why is this so tough for many business owners? There can be lots of reasons, but often the principal one is trust. Many entrepreneurial leaders just don't think they can trust their employees to do as good a job as they've done. After all, when you've developed much of the business framework, isn't it easier and quicker to do things yourself? Well, in the beginning, of course it's often easier to do it yourself. But how did you learn? How quick did you do it at the start? How's any employee going to learn if you don't give them the responsibility?

Get real. Pass over the small stuff and get working on the stuff that matters. You'll probably find – in time – that they're doing an even better job than you!

UK COMMERCIAL CLEANING

When he made an appearance in the Dragons' Den in Series 7, Tony Earnshaw demonstrated how he had built a successful business through hard work, determination and vision. He began in 2004 with a window cleaning round, rapidly made it highly profitable, then sold it so that he could aim for the larger and more lucrative commercial cleaning sector.

Having set up UK Commercial Cleaning in the Newcastle area, Tony opened a second office in Leeds just prior to his appearance in the Den and had a staff of 18. The Dragons were impressed by Tony's attitude and ambition, none more so than Duncan, who invested in the business for a 35% stake.

TOGETHER WITH *his business partner and childhood friend Stephen Pearson (left), Tony made a strong pitch in the Den.*

Because Tony is a natural leader and the driving force for his company, it has been important to instil that same ambitious mentality in his staff as the business has grown. Tony has sought to employ like-minded people, who show drive. He also believes that uniforms have a role to play, so that employees understand that they are representing the company as a whole whilst they're at work. Training is an important ingredient too, and all staff are trained to at least NVQ Level 2 when they are taken on.

Since gaining the investment from Duncan, UKCC has developed a franchising arm to grow its presence in the market more rapidly. The company is broadening its remit too, taking on deep kitchen cleaning and flood and fire restoration, and aiming to specialize in crime scene clean-ups, the removal and prevention of *C Difficile* in hospitals and the removal of bio-hazardous waste.

IT WAS OBVIOUS *from Duncan's expressions in the Den that he was keen to invest and, as he later said, recognized a kindred spirit in Tony – ambitious, determined, unstoppable.*

TONY'S COMPANY *undertakes heavy-duty industrial cleaning, as shown.*

WHY 'MANAGEMENT' ISN'T ENOUGH

Let's open out the point about leadership a little more and apply the same principles to people. There's a world of difference between managing your staff and leading them.

Managing staff is just making sure that they are doing things right. You know, re-ordering stock, making sure customers are happy, turning up every day and on time.

Leading staff is very different. It's about saying to people: this is where we're going and how we're going to get there. I want you to come with me on that journey and play a key role in helping us to reach that destination.

Now you're giving people a meaningful purpose – they connect their daily activities with the purpose of your business. Now people start doing things right: they notice a run on a particular item of stock and think, "Why's that happening?" They don't just make customers happy, they think, "What else can I do for you as a customer to make you loyal so you'll spend more with us?" They don't just turn up on time; they get in early because they know there's a big delivery coming in. They stay late because they share your passion to reach that business goal you have set.

That's real leadership. But how can we make sure you achieve this?

CHANGING YOUR LEADERSHIP STYLE

Many people say "I treat all my employees the same". But a good leader *doesn't*. If all employees were identical then the statement would be right. But you know that all employees aren't the same, so you need to learn how to use different aspects of your leadership skills in different situations.

WHEN LABAN ROOMES *(see p155) was in the Den, it was clear that he was a charismatic businessman and an individual with great drive and ambition. To paraphrase one of the Dragons, "People like dealing with you, but you need another 30 Labans to make this a scaleable business." This was the big question over Laban's gold-plating business: he had made a success of it, but, if he were to offer franchises, would others be as determined. Having obtained investment from James, Laban is more optimistic about the mutual benefits of franchising. "The development of the Goldgenie business opportunity [the franchise part of the business] means I can benefit from other people's efforts whilst still giving them a viable and profitable business opportunity, where they can not only follow my road to success but also develop much-needed skills that you only get from running your own business."*

When someone works in your business you give them two crucial things: direction and support. How much of these you give depends on each employee and the situation you find yourself in with them.

For example, if you have a new employee who is unsure of what to do and who might lack a bit of self-confidence, then what leadership style should you use? Probably one that is both clear about what tasks you need completing (direction) and reassuring that you have belief in them (support). New employees need bag-loads of both – which is why they can be time-consuming to settle in.

As people grow in ability and self-confidence, you subtly begin to change how you deal with them. With a more experienced individual you might say 'what' you'd like done but not 'how'. Their responsibility is to work out the 'how'. With highly capable employees you often just leave them to it. It's not that you don't want to carry on being supportive – but you don't want to patronize them either! If they need you, then they only have to ask.

So, to adapt your leadership style:

1 ASSESS THE SITUATION.

2 MAKE A DECISION ABOUT THE ABILITY AND CONFIDENCE LEVELS OF THE EMPLOYEE.

3 CHOOSE THE RIGHT LEADERSHIP STYLE TO SUIT THE SITUATION. Base this on how much direction and support they will need.

You don't use one style for one person either. You might have an employee who is great at dealing with customer queries. Knowing this, you leave them to it: low direction and low support. But when they chase overdue invoices they feel really unsure of themselves. This time you suggest good techniques for getting through to accounts teams (high direction) and reassure them that it soon becomes easier with practice (high support).

Think about each of your people in turn. Which style suits which employees? Take one of your employees and think about individual tasks. Which tasks can you leave them to get on with? Which tasks do they need help with?

But how is what we've discussed 'leadership'? It's leadership because every task not only builds an individual's skills (and frees you up to get on with the big stuff!) it also builds the business and gets it closer to where you want it to be.

You have a goal: you need to raise the performance of your staff so that you can achieve that goal.

" A GOOD LEADER INSPIRES OTHER MEN AND WOMEN WITH CONFIDENCE. A GREAT LEADER INSPIRES THEM WITH CONFIDENCE IN THEMSELVES. "

REED MARKHAM, SPEECH WRITER FOR THE US SUPREME COURT

EARNING RESPECT

It's strange when you consider what some people think respect is. There are those who really mean 'fear' not respect. They tyrannize staff and keep them 'in line', thinking that cowed staff will always do as they're told. But that's the problem. Staff will 'do as they're told' and do very little else. They're not going to show initiative because the fear of getting it wrong will outweigh everything.

This isn't respect – it's compliance.

Respect is about consistency and fairness, having a strong set of positive values and always demonstrating them every day.

Leaders who earn respect often gain it most by:

- **LISTENING RESPECTFULLY TO OTHERS**
- **RESPECTING OTHERS' OPINIONS**
- **RESPECTING OTHERS' NEEDS AND WANTS**
- **RESPECTING THE RIGHTS OF OTHERS**
- **RESPECTING THE DIFFERENCES IN OTHERS**

Respect is also earned by role modelling behaviour you want to see in your employees. For example, people will respect you when you hold your hand up to a decision and say, "I got that wrong."

And, finally, make sure you:

- **NEVER BETRAY A CONFIDENCE**
- **NEVER CRITICIZE SOMEONE IN FRONT OF OTHERS**
- **NEVER DO SOMETHING THAT LACKS INTEGRITY**
- **NEVER BE OVER-FAMILIAR WITH EMPLOYEES**
- **NEVER BE DISHONEST**

WHERE ARE YOU GOING?

Someone once said that management is looking after the stuff that's in the box. Leadership is about seeing where the box is going. So where is the box – that is your business – going?

If you don't know, then start deciding now! After all, what type of pilot is going to give you the most confidence on a flight? Someone who has a proper flight plan to get you towards your destination? Or one who has no idea where they're flying to or what they're going to do once they're in the air! It's the same with your employees. It's exciting to be led and helps create a real sense of meaning to work. So let's look at how we do this.

SELLING THE DREAM

Successful business people always have a purpose that is their 'point on the horizon'. Let's have a look at a couple...

- **'TO ORGANIZE THE WORLD'S INFORMATION AND MAKE IT UNIVERSALLY ACCESSIBLE AND USEFUL'** GOOGLE

- **'TO PROVIDE OUR CUSTOMERS WITH SAFE, GOOD VALUE, POINT-TO-POINT AIR SERVICES'** EASYJET

The business writer Stephen Covey stresses that it's crucial to start with the end in mind. This is what a purpose (or mission statement if that's what you prefer to call it) is trying to achieve. As a leader, you're taking them on a journey, but people will sign up much more willingly – and pay the costs of travelling with their effort and commitment – if you show them what the destination looks like.

CREATING A CULTURE

Many people believe that you can't create a culture; you can only create the right conditions and hope that the right culture emerges. Of course one of the most influential factors on any culture is the leadership style, which we've already talked about. There is many a business culture that is curdled by the personality or philosophy of the owner.

Probably the best way to create a positive culture is to decide what you think that culture should look like.

Here's an exercise for you:

IF YOU COULD IMAGINE YOUR 'PERFECT' BUSINESS...
... WHAT WOULD IT LOOK LIKE?
... HOW WOULD YOU DESCRIBE THE PHYSICAL SPACE IN WHICH PEOPLE ARE WORKING?
... WHAT ARE THE ACTIVITIES YOU SEE PEOPLE DOING?
... HOW ARE THEY TALKING WITH EACH OTHER?
... HOW WOULD YOU DESCRIBE THE ATMOSPHERE?
... WHAT IS SO DIFFERENT ABOUT WHAT YOU SEE?
... WHAT WORDS SUM UP WHAT YOU WERE ABLE TO SEE?

Write everything down. Pretty soon, you should start to see key words that describe this perfect place. These words might be 'exciting', 'buzz', 'committed', 'modern', 'traditional', 'helpful'. Now you're beginning to see what it is you need to create. The next stage would be to go to your employees and say, "This is what I want – how can we achieve it?"

An even better way of doing this exercise is getting your team together and – collectively – arriving at a set of words. These words can then become the set of values to which you hold yourself and your employees accountable. When you see people behave in a way that contradicts a value – let them know. Similarly, when they see you do something that goes against what you agreed, ask them to let you know.

RED BUTTON DESIGN

Amanda Jones and James Brown of Red Button Design appeared in the Den with designs for a water purifier and carrier for use in developing countries. The product and business have been a work in progress since, with James heading the design and development team and Amanda leading on the business model and marketing. While bringing a new innovation to the commercial market can be frustratingly time-consuming, the product (now called Midomo) is finally due to launch in late 2010.

AMANDA *now has certification from the World Health Organization for Midomo.*

Their time has not been idly spent, of course, and while James has had to tackle the technical difficulties, Amanda has had to maintain the impetus of the business without a finished product to anchor it to. In particular that means continuing to raise money to fuel the project and negotiating the web of bureaucracy that this sort of project entails. She may have had doubts over the three years, but Amanda has demonstrated a determined leadership and 2011 should open a new chapter for Red Button Design.

SPREADING THE PASSION

It's no good just thinking about having a nice set of values. You now have to demonstrate those values with your own behaviour. As the influential business writer Tom Peters has said, you have to 'Walk the Talk'. People believe what they see, not what they hear. If one of your values is honesty, then your people will notice the first time that you fail to live up to that value. Even worse, you'll not only have undermined that value – you will have effectively undermined every other value you agreed with your team.

So get passionate about the standards you want and live those standards every day, even when times are tough and you're struggling to keep things afloat. A true leader stays true to what they believe in. In the face of the sternest test, they show consistency in what they do and how they go about doing it.

BUILDING YOUR TEAM AND CREATING THE RIGHT SPIRIT

Think back to the most successful team you were ever part of. Why was it successful? What did you all do that fostered that great sense of 'team-ness'? Great teams don't just happen because a bunch of people like each other. They happen because the person who leads them makes sure that certain things are in place.

- **SUCCESSFUL TEAMS SHARE A COMMON GOAL.** Go back to the 'purpose' we were talking about earlier in the chapter.

- **SUCCESSFUL TEAMS SHARE COMMON VALUES.** Covered in 'spreading the passion' above.

- **TEAM MEMBERS COMMUNICATE.** They make sure everyone is up to speed with what's happening.

- **THEY CHALLENGE THEMSELVES.** Great teams don't stay in their comfort zones

- **THEY ARE OFTEN MADE UP OF DIFFERENT TYPES OF PEOPLE.** Coming to this one soon!

- **THEY LISTEN TO AND RESPECT EACH OTHER.** Ever been in a team full of cliques and factions? Annoying or even downright destructive, isn't it? Great teams don't actually tolerate teams within teams.

- **TEAM MEMBERS MANAGE THEMSELVES.** When the leader's away and the unexpected happens – they know what to do!

- **GREAT TEAMS MAKE WORK FUN.** Being a highly successful team is a serious business – but that doesn't mean that you have to be serious.

- **EVERYONE PLAYS A PART.** There are no freeloaders in a great team.

- **THEY CHECK THE QUALITY OF WHAT THEY DO.** Every so often they meet and assess whether there isn't a better way of doing things.

MIXING IT UP

In Commandment 7 we warned about the danger of recruiting clones of yourself. You want people around you who can do things you can't. It makes sense, after all, to widen your team's capabilities as much as you can.

But mixing it up like this can bring problems. It takes a mature leader to recognize, tolerate and value others who are different to themselves. We're not just talking gender, race and religion. We're also talking about working style, approaches to thinking and so on.

Many entrepreneurs are 'can do' people. They have already shown that when they have a dream they go right out and start working towards it. Yes, they make mistakes on the way, but they know that nothing's going to happen until you start to do something.

But how does this person cope with a thinking, reflective, cautious type? Often, not very well. Rather than value the other's approach, they casually dismiss them as 'timid' or 'over-cautious'. Maybe even a 'ditherer'. But both styles have value. Both can be even more successful if they learn to understand each other.

So you have to be tolerant of others – and set the example for others to be equally tolerant. This doesn't mean that you're a 'soft touch' and that you'll put up with unacceptable behaviour. If the cautious person misses reasonable deadlines then you've got to deal with that. But – within reason – make allowances for the style of others.

THE PERILS OF A TOO-HAPPY TEAM

Surely that's not right? You can't really have a 'too-happy' team can you? Well, yes, you can. Sometimes you need a team that challenges issues, disagrees with each other and thinks about how they can

" **REASONABLE PEOPLE ADAPT THEMSELVES TO THE WORLD. UNREASONABLE PEOPLE ATTEMPT TO ADAPT THE WORLD TO THEMSELVES. ALL PROGRESS, THEREFORE, DEPENDS ON UNREASONABLE PEOPLE.** "

GEORGE BERNARD SHAW (1856–1950), IRISH PLAYWRIGHT

'disrupt' their usual thinking. Make everything too cosy and you start to lose the good that comes out of conflict and disagreement.

Sometimes you must do this disruption yourself. Challenge what people tell you. Play 'devil's advocate' with people. Anything to stop your employees putting the harmony of the team above the quality of the team's thinking.

REMOTE AND VIRTUAL TEAMS

Often it's assumed that when you're talking about 'teams' you're talking about people who share the same building. But in today's world this isn't always the case. A **REMOTE TEAM** is one that is located in different places but all report to the same manager. A **VIRTUAL TEAM** is one that reports to different managers. Either way, these sort of teams bring the same issues and demand great things of their leader. Points to bear in mind with remote or virtual teams are:

- **GET IT RIGHT FROM THE OUTSET.** Agree clear goals, assign roles and responsibilities that everyone understands and has 'signed up' to.

" WHEN I WAS RUNNING MY OWN BUSINES I PLACED TOO MUCH EMPHASIS ON THE CONCEPT OF CONTROL. THE BETTER YOU GET AT TEAM BUILDING, THE MORE OPPORTUNITY YOU GET TO FIND A BALANCE. " JAMES CAAN, DRAGON

- **GET PEOPLE TRUSTING EACH OTHER AND WORKING TOGETHER.** Agree a set of 'ground rules' with the team and insist that people keep to them.

- **EXPLOIT THE TECHNOLOGY.** Communication is the skill your team must master. Use the great technologies out there that help you achieve this – wifi, instant messaging, video conferencing, Skype…

- **REMEMBER TIME ZONES.** Look for meeting times that suit everyone.

- **WATCH YOUR LANGUAGE.** If English isn't their first language think carefully about how you express yourself.

- **CHECK FOR UNDERSTANDING.** Have you always been understood? It never hurts to double check!

KEEPING YOUR TALENT BY DELEGATING

We started this chapter by talking about how damaging micromanaging can be, and how it often frustrates employees because they're not being trusted or allowed to develop. As you expand your business there's going to be less of you to go around and you'll need to assign tasks more and more to those you've employed.

Of course there's a right and a wrong way of doing this. A great first step is to delegate tasks to your team. Delegating has a great double whammy for a leader: not only does it give you more time to get on with the important needs of the business, it also encourages your staff to take on more responsibility. So why wouldn't anybody want to delegate? Well, usually because many entrepreneurs – as we've already said – find it very hard to let go.

Here's a delegating checklist:

- **SELECT THE RIGHT PERSON FOR THE TASK.** Have they the skills necessary to take the task over?

- **GIVE THEM PLENTY OF TIME TO DO THE TASK.** It may take them a lot longer at first to master the task.

- **EXPLAIN CLEARLY WHAT YOU WANT DOING.** Tell them when you want it done by and how the task will look when it's successfully completed.

- **AGREE A REPORTING METHOD.** How often and in what way do you want the employee to report back to you?

- **DON'T MICROMANAGE THE DELEGATED TASK!** Once it's been delegated – and you've done all of the things mentioned on the previous page – leave them to it.

OVERCOMING OBSTACLES

Leadership is so easy when everything is working fine. But once the winds gather and your business starts to get tossed by some very high waves, then you soon start seeing who the captains and passengers are. Once you have a problem on your hands then you're going to need to come up with some tough decisions. To help you make the right decision, use the following logical steps:

1   **ESTABLISH THE OBJECTIVE.** Define exactly what it is you need to achieve to get this problem solved.

2   **GENERATE GOOD ALTERNATIVES.** You and your team need to get their thinking hats on and come up with as many possible approaches and solutions as possible.

3   **EXPLORE THESE ALTERNATIVES.** Now's the time to look at the most likely solutions. What are the risks involved with each alternative? What gets you closest to the objective you decided on at the first stage?

4   **CHOOSE THE BEST ALTERNATIVE.** Select the alternative that you think will work most successfully. Draw up a 'pros and cons' grid to compare two or three alternatives to arrive at the best decision.

" YOU MUST TRUST AND BELIEVE IN PEOPLE OR LIFE BECOMES IMPOSSIBLE "

ANTON CHEKHOV (1860–1904), RUSSIAN WRITER & PHYSICIAN

5 **CHECK YOUR DECISION.** Are you sure this will solve the problem? Stress test it by asking searching questions about how well it will meet your objective.

6 **COMMUNICATE YOUR DECISION AND TAKE ACTION.** Right, get out there and put it into place. Communicate it to everyone who needs to know what's happening.

MANAGING EXPECTATIONS

In the previous Commandment we spoke about the importance of never overselling a role to an applicant. Once people are in position, it's just as important not to build up people's expectations and then fail to deliver on those expectations.

Being tactful and honest with individuals is crucial. If they have ambition but you doubt if your organization can meet them then don't make empty promises to try and keep them. Nobody is with you forever, and you have to accept that your company will be a 'stepping stone' for some to other things.

When people ask for development that is outside their role, or would be expensive to arrange, then look for a happy compromise. Always try and deal with expectations positively, but know the boundaries of what you can offer, and keep to them.

YOUDOO DOLLS

Sarah Lu leads through her creativity – her ability to innovate. She came up with the idea for the Youdoo DIY dolls, the look of the website and, as the company has grown following Deborah's investment, further Youdoo products. After gaining investment in the Den, she confided that she had roped in her aunt and friends to help make and package the dolls. She was clearly a person who could inspire those around her to get involved and feel part of her enterprise; she was also someone who could make things happen. It had taken Sarah only a matter of a few months to set up the business and start making and selling the dolls in relatively high numbers to prestigious retail clients.

AFTER APPEARING *on Dragons' Den, Sarah's sales went up about 500%. They rose again in 2008, but dropped back a little the following year. To offset the slowdown in UK sales, Sarah is pushing hard overseas, setting up distribution deals in the USA, Australia and Japan.*

Deborah's reservation about the investability of Youdoo was that the doll might be a fad – good for a Christmas or two, but with rapidly diminishing returns thereafter. It has been Sarah's role to feed the business with ideas to combat that trend, partly by introducing new products but also by reacting to and developing the community aspect of the website. The Youdoo members can upload images to a gallery and download increasing numbers of T-shirt designs for their dolls, pets and superheroes.

THE ORIGINAL YOUDOO DOLL *(top right) allowed buyers to print an image of their own face, or that of a friend or relative. Other products have followed, such as the voice recordable Youdoo Superhero (right) and Youdoo Pets, such as Youdoo Cat (below). As Sarah says, "each time a new product is produced, sales in ALL Youdoo products rise," so this is clearly a way to keep the brand evolving.*

MANAGE YOUR EXPANDING BUSINESS

Can you stay in control whilst your business grows?

MANY ENTREPRENEURIAL BUSINESSES start out from back bedrooms, garages or perhaps a corner of someone else's office. The entire business might initially take up a few square metres, with most of the administration confined to a hard drive on a computer. As you grow, however, new approaches are needed to help go from cottage industry to big business. You need to put new procedures and controls into place, and keep planning and managing the process of growth. That includes making sure your people are developing new skills to help them cope in a new business world. This Commandment puts you in the driving seat of growth, helping you to negotiate the awkward bends and corners that every expanding business faces.

BATTLING THE BUREAUCRATIC MONSTER

Success often brings expansion, but uncontrolled expansion inevitably spawns an administrative monster that just seems to create piles of paper, unopened post, a constantly blinking answering machine and gravity-defying columns of cardboard boxes. Even worse, your employees are bemused and frustrated by creaky filing systems you created in the early days of the business and that only you understand. It's time for action! Time to battle with the monster of bureaucracy and bring it to heel.

HAVING YOUR PROCESSES IN WRITING

You need to get systems in place that allow your people to work effectively, not only for the sake of efficiency but also because people like working in organizations that are genuinely well organized. Also, unless people are doing a particular process every day, they may soon forget important elements of it, and you don't want to keep reinventing the process.

What sort of processes are we talking about? It could be everything from how you handle incoming telephone calls to how you want important customers dealt with. You're not going to create procedures for how the office coffee should be made, but concentrate only on those processes that are critical to the success of your business. That covers the following:

- **COMPLICATED OR LENGTHY PROCESSES**
- **ROUTINE PROCESSES THAT MUST FOLLOW CERTAIN RULES**
- **PROCESSES THAT ARE GOING TO INVOLVE SIGNIFICANT CHANGE**

- **PROCESSES THAT MUST BE STANDARDIZED TO CREATE A CONSISTENT APPROACH**
- **PROCESSES THAT ARE GOING TO BE DOCUMENTED** (e.g. staff appraisals or perhaps a disciplinary review)

So look first for the crucial processes that your business relies on to run smoothly. Next, you're going to set up a procedure for each process, and formalize it by writing it down.

Take the following steps:

1   Decide the exact way the procedure should be done.

2   Document the procedure by setting out the process using a written explanation, developing a form, drawing up a flow chart, etc.

3   Train all of your employees who will carry out the procedure – using the documentation that you've just developed.

4   Communicate the level of authority each employee has when they use the process. Set out at what point they should escalate an issue should something go wrong.

5   Check for understanding of the procedure to make sure they feel confident with it.

WHY SYSTEMS AND PROCESSES CAN ENSLAVE STAFF

The beauty of putting your own business together is that you can make sure it doesn't get strangled by bureaucracy. Many entrepreneurs find processes and procedures a chore, worrying that they 'get in the way' of a thriving, responsive concern.

In some organizations owners have created a set of systems that would have red tape junkies weeping with envy. So it's important to remember that policies (guidelines for decision making) and procedures (the 'how-to's' for getting a job done) are meant to be the slaves of the business. Unfortunately, what happens with some businesses is the poor employees become slaves to the processes and procedures!

You have to watch for this and make sure that a procedure is there because it helps. The moment you get feedback that a procedure is pointless or unnecessary, then look carefully to decide whether the procedure is a slave of your employees – or their master.

" I'VE SEEN SO MANY BUSINESSES GET COMPLETELY BOGGED DOWN ON CAR PARKING SPACES OR WHO'S USING TOO MANY POST-IT NOTES. IF YOU DUMP THE SMALL STUFF, THEN YOU'LL FOCUS ON WHAT REALLY MATTERS TO YOUR BUSINESS. " DEBORAH MEADEN, DRAGON

PLANNING AND COMMUNICATION

The death knell for many businesses sounds – perversely – for those that are doing too well. It was probably the last problem the owner thought they'd have: business figures soaring above expectations. But uncontrolled growth, and failing to respond to it, can bring its own pains. The first port of call must be your original business plan. (You do have one, don't you?) What has been your progress since you first drew it up? Where is the business growing most?

Now's the time to reshape the original plan and map out exactly where you want the business to go and how you intend to get it there. Also, try to establish what problems your business might face if the too-rapid growth continued. Remember that if unchecked growth isn't brought under control then you risk irreparable damage to your cash flow (see Commandment 5), assets, processes and procedures, and quality control.

So let's summarize the planning and communication stages:

1   **CARRY OUT A DIAGNOSTIC ON YOUR BUSINESS.** What sort of health is it in? How can you accommodate sudden growth without damaging the business? How healthy is the current customer base? After all, this will be the central element to preventing funds for growth.

2   **IDENTIFY THE POTENTIAL OPPORTUNITIES FOR GROWTH.** What has your research told you? Which areas can you confidently expect to exploit to drive the growth? Are you growing the business by opening up new markets or by building your dominance in a particular market? What are your competitors doing?

3 **GET THE NECESSARY RESOURCES IN PLACE.** How much investment are you going to need? What will be the return on your investment and when can you have the necessary money ready? Where will be the most likely sources of funds for the growth? What other resources will you also need: staff, buildings, equipment, etc.?

4 **DEVELOP THE PLAN.** Set out the process by which you intend to grow. Stress test it thoroughly by asking 'what if?' questions at every stage.

5 **COMMUNICATE THE PLAN.** Now's the time to let your staff know what's going to be happening. Of course, you'll already have got their valuable input during much of the development of the plan itself. Your job now is to get them excited, involved and committed to its success. Is this a PR opportunity that you'll want to make use of? How about communicating your growth to the rest of the world out there?

MANAGING PEOPLE DURING A PERIOD OF GROWTH

Growth can be an exciting time for you as the business owner, but not everyone in your organization will necessarily see it your way. Existing staff especially might view the growth as threatening and

MAX MCMURDO OF REESTORE *made a successful pitch to the Dragons in Series 5, gaining investment from Deborah and Theo. With the additional funds came expansion, including taking on staff and delegating, which for someone used to working by himself proved far from easy: "I had to learn about distribution, outsourcing and ultimately trusting others. Initially, and to the Dragons' frustration, I found it very hard to let go and employ other manufacturers to take on some of the production. We have delegated a lot of the manufacturing to local fabricators, who actually do a better job than I did. (Once I learned to trust them!)"*

even secretly suspect that they may not be able to cope in this 'new world' that you've been telling them about. New people coming on board can obviously be trained directly with new procedures, but there may be friction between the original and new staff. This is where the strong leadership skills we described in Commandment 8 are really needed. You want to keep your best people, and you'll need them even more when things really take off. On the next page are some tips about introducing the idea of growth to your people.

- **LET PEOPLE KNOW WHY YOU'VE DECIDE TO GROW.** If your employees are not convinced of why you need the organization to grow then you've got big problems. Outline why you need to grow, why the original way doesn't cut it any more and what benefits growth will bring for everyone.

- **BELIEVE IN YOUR PEOPLE.** Yes, they may have doubts and look a little unsure about what you're trying to achieve, but they're a talented bunch who are key to the whole success of your business growth plan.

- **TREAT EVERYONE'S REACTIONS SENSITIVELY.** Everyone is different, so they're all going to react differently to the growth. Take people aside: listen to their fears, deal with their reservations, reassure them.

- **REMEMBER THAT GROWTH IS A PROCESS.** Let people take time to come to terms with the planned growth. Change for some is like grief; they'll come to terms with it but you shouldn't expect it to happen immediately.

- **COMMUNICATE OPENLY AND HONESTLY.** Handle people's expectations. If there are going to be problems as the organization 'beds in' to new procedures, customers or ways of doing things then let people know. Be open and honest so that you maintain the trust of your team.

MOTIVATING AND GROWING YOUR PEOPLE

Motivation is a funny thing, "a door locked on the inside" as someone once cleverly put it. People are often motivated by different things. With some the need to achieve is often as natural as breathing. They don't have a choice about wanting to make things happen – it's an uncontrollable urge that they follow.

But for others motivation comes from a different place. It could be the need to feel wanted that makes some people work so hard. With others it might be the need to achieve a status or position in life that drives them on. Your job is to find out what motivates each individual and to try and harness that energy through what you ask people to do.

Of course there are other things that keep people motivated and, more importantly, keep them working at a high level of productivity. Just making sure you do the following will maintain any employee's momentum:

- **THANK PEOPLE AND RECOGNIZE GOOD WORK.** Never under-estimate the power of a sincere 'thank you'. Even in a recession, good people are always in demand by employers. If you don't make them feel appreciated, then there are probably a lot of other businesses out there who will!

- **CHALLENGE PEOPLE WITH INTERESTING WORK.** Give them new responsibilities that help them grow. If someone's doing exactly the same job they were doing a year ago then they might feel bored or just stuck in a 'dead end'. Keep them fresh by constantly building their skills.

- **GIVE PEOPLE RESPONSIBILITY.** A great motivator for many is when they feel their work matters. Some call it the 'golden thread' that links what people do to the overall purpose of the company. This type of work provides meaning – and it's really motivating to know that what you're doing is important to everyone.

Motivation is seldom about money. Money is important but in the to and fro of everyday work it's rarely at the top of people's minds as they work.

" A DEADLINE IS A GREAT MOTIVATOR, AND WITHOUT THAT PROJECTS CAN LOSE THEIR WAY "

DUNCAN BANNATYNE, DRAGON

INVESTING IN TRAINING

In Stephen Covey's book *The 7 Habits of Highly Effective People* he tells the story of a woodcutter who is exhausted from hours of trying to cut down a tree. Someone suggests to him that he sharpens his saw, to which he replies: "I don't have time to sharpen the saw, I'm busy sawing!" It's important for everyone that, whatever job they do, they occasionally take time to 'sharpen their saw' – to work on improving their skills and make an even bigger contribution to their organization. Yet mention the word training and people instantly

AS TONY EARNSHAW'S BUSINESS, *UK Commercial Cleaning Services (see pp166–7), has grown, Tony has sought to recruit like-minded people to support the growth of his company. Specifically, "those who are passionate, driven, and who are dedicated to boosting the success of the company," as Tony puts it.*

think of a course in a hotel. But training can take many forms and sometimes the workshop in a far-off hotel is not always the best approach.

The first thing to realize is that we all like to learn in different ways. Think about it: when you unpack that new mobile phone, how do you learn to use it? Do you instantly put the battery in, turn it on and fiddle with the buttons and menus? Or do you set it aside, take out the instructions and get reading? Both are equally good ways of learning. The former is 'hands on' and the later is more 'reflective'. But just think of the frustration if you insisted that the 'hands on' learner read the manual first! It's the same when you consider training for your employees. If you're training them personally, then ask how they like to learn (remember the mobile phone example) and then train them that way. Likewise, if you need to send them on that workshop in a far-flung hotel then see what methods they will be using: 'hands on' or lots of talking heads and PowerPoint slides.

Investing in training is not just about money, though. It's also about time. If you want to train people up yourself then that's going to be a big hole in your day. You must make sure that you train people properly so that your training message sticks.

COACHING YOUR PEOPLE

Boy, do some people get confused about training and coaching. Training is all about putting skills and knowledge into people. Coaching is about bringing out of people the skills and knowledge already inside.

So why coach instead of train? Look upon training as 'telling' your employees. Of course you have to do this, but what if you were to do this all the time? Eventually your staff would sit around all day waiting to be told what to do. Rather than using their initiative and sorting issues out for themselves, they would wait until they could ask you because that's the relationship your constant telling has created.

What you need to do is to build independence in your staff so that, when you are away from the premises or just difficult to get hold of, they'll know what they should do.

So start coaching them. When they ask you a question ask them what they believe the answer might be. If their response isn't the correct one then give them a hint or ask another question that helps them work it out ('what' questions are always the best). What you're really doing for your employee is getting them to think for themselves and to stop looking to you as the 'guru' who is always there to answer the smallest query.

The beauty of this approach is that you're building accountability in people. You're asking them to be responsible for thinking about their work and making decisions that will give them the confidence to be more independent.

Just think about it: if people were able to get on with doing their own work and not keep firing endless questions at you, how many more hours in a week would you be creating?

MANAGING UNDERPERFORMERS

Of course, when you start to take people through change, you may find that some staff really struggle to cope. This can show itself in different ways; for example, you may notice that an employee's work is not up to standard. But why is this happening? Is it because they can't produce the work you need – or is it because they won't? The first factor may be capability; the second is probably going to be conduct. Let's look at both.

CAPABILITY

You start to realize that the person just isn't demonstrating the ability to do the job. This would be completely expected of a new employee, but if you have someone who's been in the job long enough to have mastered the skills, then you need to ask yourself are they capable?

You must ask yourself some searching questions when you have capability issues. Be honest: has anyone ever sat down with them and told them exactly what they need to be doing, why and to what standard? If not, then it's certainly not fair to criticize them for not getting it right. Also, will some training help? Could that bring them up to standard? Is there something going on that you don't know about? A difficulty at home? Money problems? A difficult work colleague even?

Don't just jump in on this one. What you must do – and this will help you later on should it all turn nasty and legal – is give support and training to help them come up to standard. By the way, make sure you keep records of what was done and when, because you may need these later on.

CONDUCT

With conduct what you're witnessing is someone who is not behaving to the standards you require. Of course this word covers a lot of behaviour, from minor mood swings right up to taking a swing at a customer!

Persistent misconduct usually leads to disciplinary action. This is where you need to have some key documents in place: a performance review procedure and a staff handbook setting out exactly what that procedure is and what you mean by words such as 'gross misconduct'. Dealing with conduct takes a lot of patience, assertion and tact.

If you find that you have either of the above issues then you might want to turn to others for advice. A good starting place is the **ACAS** website (www.acas.org.uk) which will certainly bring you up to speed on the legal niceties of what you're encountering.

You may also want to think about a human resources specialist or legal counsel. Whatever you do, as soon as you suspect that an issue is beginning to develop: take advice! One false step with many of these types of issues can be very expensive and, for matters related to discrimination and harassment, possibly fatal to your business.

THE EMPLOYEE HANDBOOK

Part of being a 'grown up' company is having all of the policies and documents in place for your staff. On p161 we mentioned that you must draw up a contract of employment for permanent staff within two months of them starting, which can include your policies on health and safety, absence etc. Other policies and documents that you may want to think about implementing might include:

- EMPLOYEE HANDBOOK DETAILING INTERNAL PROCEDURES
- COMPUTER USE, EMAILS AND COMMUNICATIONS POLICY
- EQUAL OPPORTUNITIES AND HARASSMENT POLICY
- ENVIRONMENTAL POLICY
- DISCIPLINARY AND GRIEVANCE PROCEDURE
- DRUGS AND ALCOHOL MISUSE POLICY
- WHISTLE-BLOWING POLICY

You can wrap up all the above in the 'Employee Handbook'. Such a document must be clearly written, not too long and not stuffed with off-putting legal jargon. You can of course develop the policies yourself but many business owners prefer to get them from organizations that specialize in supplying ready-made documents that can be easily customized. Type 'employment policies' into a search engine for links to companies providing these.

CUDDLEDRY

When Helen Wooldridge and Polly Marsh appeared in the Den, they were seeking investment of £100,000 for a company that they'd launched some nine months earlier. Their business was on a sound footing. They had orders from independent and chain stores in the UK, had the manufacturing located in China to keep production costs low, and were making a 100% mark-up between manufacturing costs and the wholesale price.

However, their projected figures had underestimated the real overhead costs: they had not accounted for full salaries and were currently dependent on unpaid help from friends and family. These and other hidden costs had the knock-on effect of

HELEN WOOLDRIDGE AND POLLY MARSH
demonstrating the Cuddledry product to the Dragons in 2007.

exaggerating the size of profits and, therefore, the overall value of their business. Like many entrepreneurs starting up a company, Helen and Polly seemed focused more on the product than the business.

Taking this into account, two Dragons were still prepared to make them the offer, but asked for 40% and 45% respectively.

Cuddledry were prepared to offer no more than 35% and so left without the investment.

Since then, their sales have been even better than they had projected and the duo have a very profitable company. With the business having now been running successfully for three years, they are looking towards an exit strategy that will see them selling the business in about Year 6, releasing money to start a new business, with the aim of being 'serial entrepreneurs' in the future.

THE BUSINESS HAS EXPANDED *into new markets globally and increased the range of its products, from the Cuddledry baby towel original (below) to robes for older children and towels for pets (above). The Cuddledry team now includes 11 people, including admin staff, national and international accounts managers, a marketing manager and several agents.*

GET BIG OR GET OUT

Will you keep growing or stage an exit?

HEALTHY BUSINESSES continue to grow. It is almost a natural law. How quickly and how big a business grows depends on a number of strategic decisions. The first nine Commandments of this book have focused largely on how to handle internal or 'organic' growth. This final Commandment looks at external methods of growth such as joint development and acquisition strategies. Alternatively, a business can grow by focusing on core operations and 'getting out' (or disposing) of non-core operations. Finally, we look at exit routes for 'getting out' of (or selling) a business.

JOINT DEVELOPMENT STRATEGIES

You can team up with people outside your business in order to grow, through franchising, licensing, strategic alliances and joint ventures.

JOINT DEVELOPMENT STRATEGIES – FRANCHISING

Franchising achieves growth through others. In return for an initial franchise fee and a monthly royalty the franchisee receives a proven business concept, a brand, training and business support. Typical franchise agreements include advertising arrangements, equipment leasing and the supply of private label products. A franchisor juggles many balls – running their existing business, looking after existing franchisees and selling new franchises to fuel growth.

A POPULAR PROMOTIONAL SLOGAN TO RECRUIT FRANCHISEES IS 'BEING IN BUSINESS FOR YOURSELF BUT NOT BY YOURSELF'

In practice almost anything can be franchised – coaching, coffee, energy audits, dating, fitness, gardening, golf, pet care, senior care and tyre sales, to name a few. Two of the most well-known franchises are McDonald's and The Body Shop. A notable example from Dragons' Den was Razzamataz (see right), whose owner, Denise, Hutton, requested £50,000 of investment to expand her drama, dance and singing school franchise. Before securing her investment from Duncan Bannatyne she faced a 25-minute battle in the Den.

DENISE HUTTON, THE FOUNDER OF RAZZAMATAZ, *pitched for her children's performing arts franchise business in Series 4. Typically the business had started small – one school with three teachers and 25 children attending. Denise opened a few more schools across the north of England and in Scotland, then looked at the franchise route to grow the business more rapidly. What's interesting about the case of Razzamataz is that there was already a major competitor called Stagecoach with a similar and very successful franchise business. They had approximately 600 schools nationwide at the time of Denise's pitch. For some Dragons, Richard Farleigh in particular, this was enough to put him off investing. Stagecoach was bigger and more established. Duncan, however, saw things differently. He had invested in Stagecoach and knew how the business operated; he had also made a very good return on his investment with them. He saw that, with a network of very local groups (as is the case with theatre schools), there was room for both businesses to grow and thrive without stepping on each other's toes, so to speak. That has proved to be the case, and Razzamataz now has schools throughout England and Scotland, and, as with Stagecoach, is expanding internationally too.*

MICHAEL LEA *made the preparations for a franchise operation prior to going in the Den, but, in the end, decided that the timing wasn't right. He's put his plans on ice, whilst testing the water with a couple of franchisees (see p212–13).*

Theo Paphitis reacted explosively when Denise said she wanted some of the money to help franchisees finance their franchises. He exclaimed that the whole point of a franchise was that franchisees are motivated to succeed as they invest their own capital.

PROS AND CONS OF FRANCHISING

- **MOTIVATION AND RESOURCES.** Organic expansion relies on having motivated employees, as we've covered in earlier chapters. Franchisees have the ultimate motivation because they are owners of their own franchise. A franchise combines a business's strength with the motivation and financial resources of individual entrepreneurs.

- **FAST ROUTE TO GROWTH.** For businesses with a credible track record of offering a unique product or service, franchising is one of the quickest and fastest ways to grow.

- **BIG BUSINESS.** One out of ten businesses in the US is a franchise. In the UK franchising accounts for £10.8 billion of sales annually, and the number of franchise units has grown by 44% over the last decade.

- **EASILY COPIED.** Despite the success of franchising, it's difficult to establish a viable and profitable business model that cannot be easily copied by competitors but can be easily implemented by your franchisees.

The British Franchise Association (www.thebfa.org) is a useful resource of information and holds regular seminars.

JOINT DEVELOPMENT STRATEGIES – LICENSING

Licensing is where a licensor sells, for a fixed fee or royalty, the rights to exploit an 'asset', typically within a geographical area. Licenses can be granted over:

- **A PRODUCT, BRAND OR ARTWORK**, such as comic book characters.

- **A PRODUCTION PROCESS**, for example a soft drink recipe.

- **MANUFACTURING OR TECHNOLOGICAL KNOW-HOW**, for example computer software.

- **INTELLECTUAL PROPERTY**, for example a television programme like Dragons' Den...

HAVING TAKEN THE iTEDDY TO MARKET *and proved it to be a big seller in Argos, the entrepreneur Imran Hakim soon decided to license the manufacture and sale of the toy in order to free up his time for other ventures (see pp226–7).*

Calvin Klein is an example of licensing. As much of 90% of the company's profits come from licensing its perfumes and underwear and jeans. The rest comes from its line of women's designer clothing.

Like franchising, licensing is a fast and profitable method of business growth. The licensor receives additional revenue with little associated cost. The cost of expansion is borne by licensees, who use their own production systems, marketing channels and distribution infrastructure. Whilst the royalty percentage is relatively small, the profits can grow very quickly. Alternatively, you can achieve growth by becoming a licensee of a product or service that complements your existing offering.

In practice license agreements are complex and vary in their constraints as well as royalty percentages. Managing the legalities behind the contracts as well as associated patents and trademarks requires specialist legal advice. The International Licensing Industry Merchandisers' Association (www.licensing.org) has information.

JOINT DEVELOPMENT STRATEGIES – STRATEGIC ALLIANCES

A strategic alliance is where two or more businesses achieve synergy through collaboration. For example, joint marketing campaigns, advertising to each other's customers, sharing rent and forming a purchasing consortium.

Strategic alliances can work especially well for small businesses. For example, alliances between wedding planners and florists; graphic designers and printers; building contractors and landscapers; estate agents, mortgage brokers and interior decorators.

Toshiba built itself as a global semiconductor player through forming strategic alliances to generate new technology it could not have developed on its own. It formed an alliance with General Electric to co-produce micro-filaments for light bulbs and it joined hands with Siemens and IBM in joint research of semiconductors.

Strategic alliances are less formal than a joint venture or acquisition and can simply be an agreement to work together. Each business retains its individual corporate identity. They can be a useful method of testing relationships before a joint venture or merger.

If you are forming a strategic alliance with other businesses make sure you formally agree on issues such as financial investment and risk, split of revenue, ownership of jointly created intellectual property and branding, and your exit strategy.

EARLE'S SANDWICHES

When he stepped into the Den in 2009, Michael Lea had already been in business with a mobile food service for office workers for 12 years. The business was profitable, and now he wanted to expand the operational hours of his vehicles. They had been selling coffee and breakfast snacks from 8.00am, continuing into lunchtime sandwiches and drinks up until about 1.30pm. But simply with the addition of an ice cream machine, they could stay out longer, having, as Michael put it, "a second bite at the cherry" in the afternoon.

However, rather than simply expanding his business by putting ice cream machines into his existing vehicles,

MICHAEL *is currently trialling two franchises. If they go well, he still plans to expand that part of his business in the future.*

Michael had decided to set up a separate company to sell franchises of his trading model and bespoke vehicle, lessening his responsibility in the day-to-day running of lots of vehicles. He had invested £160,000 of his own money into the new venture and was seeking a further £100,000 from the Dragons to take it forward.

Michael got an offer in the Den, but later both parties felt the timing wasn't right. With the economy in recession and banks less willing to loan to individuals wanting to buy franchises, Michael decided to scale back his initial plans to set up 50 in rapid succession.

He is currently trialling two franchises to monitor how well they work. If they prove to be successful, he'll then be able to provide banks with convincing figures and case histories when future prospective franchisees seek loans to set up in business.

PETER OFFERED MICHAEL *a deal that would include having a stake in Michael's existing sandwich business as well as the franchise venture. The offer required careful consideration.*

ALTHOUGH A DEAL *was struck in the Den, both parties felt in subsequent months that the timing wasn't right for a major franchise operation.*

JOINT DEVELOPMENT STRATEGIES – JOINT VENTURES

A joint venture (JV) is where two or more businesses join forces and set up a new business as separate legal entity.

A joint venture can be 'vertical' (with a supplier or customer) or 'horizontal' (pooling resources with a business in the same niche). For example, a printing company could a form a vertical joint venture with an ink manufacturer or a book publisher. Alternatively it could form a horizontal joint venture with a stationery supply store to create a bigger pool of products and services to be offered to a wider base of customers.

Many businesses use joint ventures to expand geographically, more quickly and cheaply than they could on their own. For example, Tesco, the third largest retailer in the world, has used several joint ventures to achieve growth. Tesco Bank was originally a joint venture with RBS. Tesco Mobile is a joint venture with O2. Tesco has also used joint ventures internationally, for example in South Korea, Malaysia and Thailand.

A small, growing company could form a joint venture with a mature, cash-rich company to exploit innovative products, intellectual property or cutting-edge technology.

The Cambridge Phenomenon is associated with academic spin-off joint ventures, established to exploit intellectual property created within university laboratories. The region around The Fens, Cambridge, England is known as 'Silicon Fen' due to the success of many of these high-tech businesses.

Finding suitable joint venture partners can be a challenge. Trade seminars and conferences might be useful places to start looking for appropriate partners. You could also approach customers, suppliers

"I'VE ACTUALLY MADE THE MAJORITY OF MY MONEY DURING TIMES WHEN THINGS HAVE BEEN TOUGH. I PERSONALLY LIKE TOUGH TIMES." THEO PAPHITIS, DRAGON

and even competitors. Joint venture business brokers can match suitable businesses together in return for a fee.

As with any partnership, it is important to make formal agreements in advance. For example, agreements about the balance of power and share of profits. Many joint ventures fail and lead to expensive break-ups due to a lack of commitment and conflicting goals between partners. Concert Communications Services – an infamous joint venture between BT and a number of other telecom providers – stalled a number of times and eventually finished in 2000, due to poor relationships.

ACQUISITION STRATEGIES

The ultimate way to achieve fast growth is through mergers and acquisitions (M&As). Although the terms are often used interchangeably, an acquisition and merger are technically different.

ACQUISITIONS

An acquisition is usually where a larger business (an acquirer) purchases a smaller business (a target). Post-acquisition, the target becomes part of the acquirer.

Google has acquired many smaller businesses, from multi-billion dollar acquisitions, like YouTube, to many smaller ones, like Tonic Systems, which provided a competitive product to Microsoft's Powerpoint.

Whilst there are many large and high-profile acquisitions, such as Kraft Foods' acquisition of Cadbury in 2010, there are also many lower-profile acquisitions of small businesses, which represent a major source of growth for acquirers.

A cash-rich business that makes wise acquisitions during a recession, when valuations are low, can grow quickly once the economy recovers.

MERGERS

A merger is when two businesses of similar sizes and operations join forces to create a single entity that combines their strengths and creates both synergies and economies of scale.

A good example of a high-profile merger is GlaxoSmithKline plc, the world's second-largest pharmaceutical company, which was formed from the merger of GlaxoWellcome and SmithKline Beecham in 2000.

TYPICAL BENEFITS OF MERGERS & ACQUISITIONS

- **REVENUE SYNERGIES** – access to new assets; intellectual capital; brands; products; services; customers; cross selling opportunities; sales teams; sales methodologies and increased market share.

- **MANAGEMENT SYNERGIES** – access to skilled employees; their knowledge; methods of working; and the sharing of ideas.

- **COST SYNERGIES** – economies of scale; increased purchasing power; and the elimination of duplicate assets, products and costs (although this can often cause employee morale problems if not handled appropriately).

- **FINANCIAL SYNERGIES** – complementary cash flow cycles; access to financial resources; tax benefits; and the ability to raise cheaper finance.

- **THE ELIMINATION OF A COMPETITOR** – where a competitor is acquired.

TYPICAL PROBLEMS OF MERGERS & ACQUISITIONS

Despite the advantages of M&As, many subsequently fail for reasons such as the following:

- **NO BENEFIT.** Ideally an acquisition will be conducted and negotiated on mutually beneficial terms. However, where the acquisition is 'hostile' and 'contested' by the target business, the price paid for the business can often exceed the benefits from any synergies. Therefore, finding a friendly target can make a big difference.

- **INSUFFICIENT 'DUE DILIGENCE'** (an investigation and evaluation of a potential partner). The target business may not be a good fit or its true financial situation may not have been apparent in its financial statements.

- **POOR INTEGRATION.** Integration of employees, infrastructure, operating systems and culture can be disastrous if not properly planned and managed. Poor integration has led to many failed M&As.

- **ADVERSE STAKEHOLDER REACTION.** The reaction of key shareholders, customers, suppliers and employees should be considered before an acquisition. Ideally they should be consulted early on and kept informed throughout.

- **MANAGEMENT DISTRACTION.** Planning, negotiations and integration require considerable management time. However, business continues and competitors don't wait.

- **INAPPROPRIATE FINANCE.** Acquisitions and their integration can absorb much needed finance that can takes years to recover. For example, the financing of the Malcolm Glazer's gradual takeover of Manchester United in 2003–5 was controversially financed by large amounts of debt.

Business brokers can help to identify goals, pre-screen possible targets, be on hand to advise on offers, and facilitate closing deals.

PROWASTE

Paul Tinton of Prowaste gained investment in the Den in Series 6. It is often assumed that it'll be plain sailing once such a deal has been struck, but the truth is that it took eight months of negotiating to iron out the details. Eighteen months later, however, Paul concludes that "it was the best decision we ever made".

PROWASTE *remains true to its core business aim, which can be summed up succinctly as 'Recycle More. Landfill Less.'*

Paul meets once a month with his Dragon investors, Deborah and Duncan, to discuss key decisions and strategy. One of the first key strategies was to relocate the business to London (one of Paul's principal aims in the pitch). Since then – and despite an economic downturn that has hit the building trade particularly hard – Prowaste's turnover has more than doubled.

Having consolidated their presence in London, Prowaste is currently expanding its reach by launching a National Skip Hire Service to residential and smaller trade waste customers throughout the UK. Whilst looking for new ways to grow, Paul's core mission remains the same: to explore and develop sustainable solutions to the problems of waste.

"WHENEVER YOU HIT A SUMMIT, THERE IS ALWAYS ANOTHER MOUNTAIN TO CLIMB. I'VE NEVER RUN OUT OF CHALLENGES."

JAMES CAAN, DRAGON

DEMERGING TO FOCUS ON THE CORE

A business can actually grow by becoming smaller! Many businesses become unwieldy and lose sight of their core mission. Others have strongly performing products which are dragged down by the rest of the business. Therefore, a rationalization of the product portfolio, retaining only high-growth core products, can produce a faster-growing, more profitable business.

Typical reasons to 'de-merge' parts of a business are to:

- REGAIN FOCUS ON THE CORE MISSION
- CONSOLIDATE GEOGRAPHICALLY
- REDUCE OVERHEADS AND EXPENSES AND CUT AWAY BUREAUCRACY AND EXCESS
- REDUCE DEBT
- REALIZE FUNDS, WHICH CAN BE USED TO PURSUE AN ALTERNATIVE STRATEGY
- REALIZE THE HIDDEN VALUE OF A BUSINESS UNIT

An example of demerging is Kraft Foods, which has made clear it is prepared to dispose of lower-margin, low-growth parts of the business to grow its overall business. As well as selling its frozen pizza business in 2010 (partly to fund the £10bn bid for Cadbury), Kraft sold its Post Cereal group in 2007. Post was a low-growth business with limited margins, which was exposed to increasing competition from private label retailer brands.

In another example, in 2010 Liberty International plc demerged its £6.1bn property empire into two separate companies. One (Capital Shopping Centres) to focus on relatively low-risk shopping centres and the other (Capital and Counties) to focus on the relatively higher-risk longer-term London estate. Patrick Burgess, Liberty chairman, has said: "[The two companies] will be positioned to execute their own strategic plans, engaging with investors who will be able to select their individual weightings to each of the businesses." Shareholders will be able to realize more value from two separate businesses than one consolidated business.

SELLING YOUR BUSINESS

At the end of the journey is selling the business. Wise entrepreneurs often plan their exit strategy before they start a business, whether it's to retire or to use the proceeds to start their next business.

There are four stages to selling a business. First you need to prepare the business itself for sale – a bit like sprucing up a house before you invite round the estate agents. Then you need to prepare a valuation and consider the best timing for putting it up for sale. Then you need to find a buyer. We'll look at these stages in turn.

CUDDLEDRY'S OWNERS, *Polly Marsh and Helen Wooldridge, were initially focused on the product (see pp202–3). As sales grew, they focused on the prosperity of the business and as that developed they looked to the medium-term future, considering what they wanted out of life. They decided then on an exit strategy of selling the business in a few years' time in order to start the process all over again with a new business venture.*

HOW TO PREPARE YOUR BUSINESS FOR SALE

- **ENSURE THE BUSINESS IS FINANCIALLY STRONG.** In the years prior to the sale, strengthen the balance sheet and ensure key ratios, such as the ratio of assets to liabilities (see Commandment 5) look healthy.

- **PREPARE FORECASTS FOR SALES AND PROFITS.** Again, see Commandment 5.

- **BE CLEAR ON THE REASONS FOR SALE.** You must be able to assure buyers they are not purchasing a 'sinking ship'.

"YOU VALUE YOUR COMPANY AT £1 MILLION. WHAT PLANET ARE YOU ON? "

JAMES CAAN, DRAGON, TO ENTREPRENEUR IN THE DEN

- **DOCUMENT KEY SYSTEMS AND PROCESSES, TO AID DUE DILIGENCE.**

- **BALANCE THE INFORMATION.** Release enough information to tempt prospective buyers whilst keeping competitively valuable information secure. (For example, in preparing information for prospective buyers, the owners of a highly successful bakery should not feel obliged to give away the secret ingredient that makes its cakes so delicious and sought after.)

HOW TO PREPARE A VALUATION

Essentially, a business is worth what someone is willing to pay for it. However, some established techniques can give indicative values. Valuing a business is an art, and professionals can help determine an appropriate value.

- For most businesses, a **MULTIPLE OF HISTORIC OR FORECAST PROFITS** will provide the best valuation. As an alternative, revenue multiples can be used for businesses with fluctuating profits or even losses.

- A **DISCOUNTED CASH-FLOW VALUATION** is statistically sound and most appropriate for a mature cash-generative business.

- An **ASSET-BASED VALUATION** is a useful minimum benchmark of a business's value; however this method does not fully reflect future growth potential as balance sheet values are usually based on historic costs. Asset-based valuations work best for businesses with high-value assets, such as property or manufacturing equipment.

Be aware that none of the valuations produced are likely to be the final price paid by a buyer. The techniques above merely supply a range of values, which can be used by buyers and sellers as a starting point for negotiations. The **FINAL VALUATION** will depend upon:

- The strategic reasons for buying or selling.
- The number of competing buyers and sellers.
- The negotiation skills of both buyers and sellers.
- The state of the economy.
- If the purchase price is paid in cash or in shares.
- Where there are multiple owners – if all agree to the sale.
- If the valuation is for the whole or part of a business.

The objective of most sellers is to maximize the valuation but at the same time the objective of most buyers is to minimize the valuation. To attract the most buyers the valuation should be as fair as possible.

GETTING THE TIMING RIGHT

A business will attract the highest valuation and is more likely to attract multiple offers when it is performing well.

Selling a business close to its year end may secure a higher valuation based on current earnings, which are mostly in the bag, rather than on the previous year's historic earnings.

FINDING A BUYER

Business brokers can help pre-screen possible buyers, narrow the field, help with negotiations and assist with paperwork. Your local Chambers of Commerce (www.britishchambers.org.uk) or Business Link (www.businesslink.gov.uk) or trade associations are useful places to start the search for potential buyers.

Online marketplaces are used to sell many businesses. Daltons (www.daltonsbusiness.com) is said to be the UK's largest. Another, Businesses for Sale (www.businessesforsale.com), includes international opportunities. Online marketplaces are also useful to research potential targets (see Acquisition Strategies earlier in this chapter).

"MY ATTITUDE TO LIFE IS WHAT'S NEXT, WHAT'S NEXT, WHAT'S NEXT... "

DEBORAH MEADEN, DRAGON

iTEDDY

It was a very rapid ascent for Imran Hakim, from coming up with the idea of iTeddy to selling the toys internationally. He pitched the idea in 2007, when he had no more than the bare bones of a prototype, designs for the toy's eventual look and a vision about how it could eventually function with movie and story downloads from a dedicated website.

ACCORDING TO PETER JONES, *Imran is the Dragons' Den's first investment millionaire.*

Dragon Duncan was saddened by the idea that a parent could be replaced by a teddy that told bedtime stories, but Peter and Theo saw the potential and jointly offered the investment. Within a few months, iTeddies were being manufactured in the Far East and an exclusive retail deal had been set up with Argos – it became one of their bestselling toys in 2007. It was still an early stage of the business and Imran was having to oversee production as well get to grips with the marketing and distribution in a market that was new to him.

Imran then did a deal with the UK's biggest independent toy manufacturer, Vivid

Imaginations, so that he could take a more back-seat role. Vivid acquired the rights to make and sell the iTeddy, handling production, marketing and distribution. As Imran said at the time, "they've taken a whole weight off my shoulders".

While retaining an interest in iTeddy, Imran is now fixed on the future and business opportunities still to come. As Theo said, "Imran is one of those guys that you can see

THE iTEDDY, *with its built-in media player.*

looks forward ... everything he does, he thinks of the next stage." He and Imran are both convinced that they will work together again on other projects. "This has got to be the most exciting thing I've done in my life, and it doesn't seem to be ending," said Imran. "Long may that continue."

DESPITE HAVING ONLY A RUDIMENTARY PROTOTYPE *to show, Imran made an assured presentation because he had done his homework on the potential market.*

REFERENCE

DOS AND DON'TS

1 **DO BE CLEAR ABOUT WHETHER YOU REALLY WANT TO GROW OR NOT.** Growth does not always bring greater profit. Indeed, rapid expansion can be one of the main causes of death for businesses. You must work out if growing is going to be right for you personally.

2 **DON'T OVERLOOK ALTERNATIVE WAYS TO GROW.** Simply selling more of what you already sell is not the only way to grow. There may be areas of the marketplace you can tap into that will augment your original core business.

3 **DO LOOK FOR GAPS IN THE MARKET.** See if you can identify any gaps – geographical areas, products, price points, channels, business models, brand extensions, and so on – that are not already being exploited.

4 **DO LOOK AT SELLING CHANNELS.** You might be able to sell more through different outlets, ranging from mail order to affiliate schemes, at a relatively low risk.

5 **DON'T LET CASH FLOW PROBLEMS SINK YOU.** You will need to handle more complex accounting procedures as you expand. Make sure you thoroughly understand budgets, the cash operating cycle, and how to control both short-term and long-term solvency and stability.

6 **DO CONSIDER ALL OPTIONS FOR FINANCING.** Now that you're an established business, you may find you have more finance options than when you first started up. Compare the pros and cons of each.

7 **DON'T SADDLE YOURSELF WITH THE WRONG PEOPLE.** You want to attract and keep good workers for your growing business, so you must prepare thoroughly for interviewing a shortlist of candidates, and make sure the vacancies are a genuinely attractive proposition for them.

8 **DO BECOME A LEADER, NOT A MICROMANAGER.** In an expanding business, you simply won't have enough hours in the day to oversee your people's every move. Learn the skills of team-building and leadership.

9 **DON'T STICK RIGIDLY TO THE OLD PROCEDURES.** The systems that suited your start-up business may need to be adapted as you grow larger. Formal documentation and training will probably become more important.

10 **DO WORK OUT YOUR LONG-TERM STRATEGY.** Decide if you want to continue growing, such as through franchising or acquiring or merging with other companies, or if you want to sell the business as an exit strategy.

JARGON BUSTER

ANGEL INVESTOR

Private investor who can provide expertise as well as capital.

ANSOFF MATRIX

Marketing term for four classic ways to expand.

ASSETS

Money, equipment and other valuables owned by a business.

CAPITAL

Money invested in a business, for example share capital.

CASH FLOW / CASH OPERATING CYCLE

The movement of money in and out of a business over a given period.

CREDIT

Broadly, receiving goods or services in advance of payment.

DIRECT COSTS

Costs directly related to providing goods or a service.

EMPLOYER'S LIABILITY INSURANCE

Compulsory form of insurance if you recruit staff.

EMPLOYMENT POLICIES

Formal documentation for employees on subjects such as equal opportunities, health & safety, maternity, absence and disciplinary procedures.

EQUITY

Portion of a company's assets owned by shareholders: equal to total assets minus liabilities.

FINANCE

Raising money through debt or selling equity. More broadly, the management of money.

GEARING / LEVERAGE

Measure of a business's long-term financing arrangements.

LIABILITIES

A business's debts and other potential outgoings.

LIQUIDITY

Ability of an asset to be converted quickly into cash.

OPERATING EXPENSES / OVERHEADS

Day-to-day costs of running a business, such as administration.

OVERCAPITALIZATION

Assets that are not being used effectively.

OVERTRADING

Imbalance between the work or orders a business receives and its ability to provide it.

PRODUCT LIFE CYCLE

The normal cycle of conception, growth, maturity, decline and death of any product or technology.

PROFIT MARGIN

The gross margin is the difference between revenue and direct costs; the net margin takes overheads too.

ROI

Return on Investment – a measure of profitability.

SOLVENCY

Ability to cover liabilities.

VALUATION

Indication of the value of a business to potential buyers.

VENTURE CAPITALIST

Professional investor who provides capital in return for equity in companies with high potential growth.

CREDITS

Produced by Thameside Media
www.thamesidemedia.com

Creative Director & Photographer:
  Michael Ellis
Editorial Director: Rosalyn Ellis
Assistant Photographer: Sergio Zimerman
Proofreader and Indexer: Zoe Ross

DRAGONS' DEN

Dragons' Den and all associated logos,
images and trade marks are owned and/or
controlled by 2waytraffic, a Sony
Entertainment company/CPT Holdings

Product Director: Lisa O'Connell
Licensing Director: David Christopher

The publishers would like to thank Sam
Lewens, Holly Simpson, Helen Bullough
and Richard Curwen at the BBC, and the
team at 2waytraffic.

Thameside Media would like to thank all
the Dragons' Den entrepreneurs who
kindly provided their assistance:

Iain McGill and Joe Gill of About Time;
Michael Pritchard of Anyway Spray; Ed
Wray at BarbeSkew; Richard Enion and
Michael Davis of BassToneSlap; Frank
Drewett of Bin Lid Lifter; Simeone Salik,
Janice Dalton and Dominic Lawrence of
Blinds In A Box; Charlotte Evans and
Carolyn Jarvis of Buggyboot; Eddie
Middleton at Chillchasers; Helen
Wooldridge and Polly Marsh of
Cuddledry; Julia Charles of D4M;
Michael Cotton of DDN; Clive Billing
of Diamond Geezer; Josephine Buchan
of Dusty; Michael Lea of Earle's Direct;
Eglu; Sammy French of Fit Fur Life;
Laban Roomes of Goldgenie; Peter Neath
and Ian Worton of Grillstream; Eoin
O'Mahony at Hamfatter; Shane Lake and
Tony Charles of Hungry House; Alistair
Turner at Igloo; Imran Hakim of iTeddy;
Joe Reade at Island Bakery Organics;
Karen O'Neill and Karen Coombes of
KCO Iceblading; Dr Gili Kucci of Kucci
Kukui; Geoff and Rob Hill of Ladderbox;
Raymond Smith of Magic Pizza; Neil
Westwood at Magic Whiteboard; Sharon
Wright of Magnamole; David and Patti
Bailey of Motormouse; Carol Savage of
MyDish; Victoria McGrane of Neurotica;
Michael North, The Olive Man; Paul
Ward of Paragon PE; Kay Russell of
Physicool; Levi Roots of Reggae Reggae
Sauce; Paul Tinton of Prowaste; Guy
Portelli; Andy Harsley of Rapstrap;
Red Button Design; Max McMurdo of
Reestore; Samantha Gore of Saboteur;
Toby and Oliver Richmond of Servicing
Stop; Samantha Fountain of Shewee;
Lesley-Ann Simmons of Shoes Galore;
Jane Rafter of Slinks; Ronan McCarthy of
Spit 'n' Polish Shoeshine; Shaun Pulfrey of
Tangle Teezer; Jason Roberts of Tech 21;
Rachel Watkyn of Tiny Box Company;
Steve Smith of trueCall; Rob Law at
Trunki; Sarah Lu of Youdoodoll; Tony
Earnshaw of UK Commercial Cleaning;
Huw Gwyther of Visual Talent; Adejare
Doherty of The Wholeleaf Company

Case studies compiled by
Thameside Media

For the official Dragons' Den website, see
www.bbc.co.uk/dragonsden

PICTURE CREDITS
Jacket photography and chapter opener
images of the Dragons' Den by
Thameside Media

Images of entrepreneurs' products and
premises kindly supplied by the businesses
named

Image of Evan Davis, p10, provided by
HarperCollins

FURTHER ADVICE
Stuart Warner's website
www.financial-fluency.co.uk

Peter Spalton's website
www.spalton.co.uk

Michael Heath's website
www.mhconsult.com

Business Link provides free business
advice and support in the UK
Helpline 0845 600 9006
www.businesslink.gov.uk

ALSO IN THIS SERIES
Dragons' Den: Start Your Own Business
(Collins, 2010) ISBN 978-0007364282

Dragons' Den: The Perfect Pitch
(Collins, 2010) ISBN 978-0007364275

FURTHER READING
Dragons' Den: Success, From Pitch To Profit
(Collins, 2008) ISBN 978-0007270828

Duncan Bannatyne *Anyone Can Do It:
My Story* (Orion, 2007) ISBN 978-
0752881898

Duncan Bannatyne *Wake Up and
Change Your Life* (Orion, 2009)
ISBN 978-0752882871

Duncan Bannatyne *How To Be
Smart With Your Money* (Orion, 2009)
ISBN 978-1409112860

Duncan Bannatyne *How To Be Smart
With Your Time* (Orion, 2010)
ISBN 978-1409112884

James Caan *The Real Deal* (Virgin, 2009)
ISBN 978-0753515099

Peter Jones *Tycoon* (Hodder, 2008)
ISBN 978-0340952351

Deborah Meaden *Common Sense Rules*
(Random House, 2010)
ISBN 978-1847940278

Theo Paphitis *Enter the Dragon* (Orion,
2009) ISBN 978-0752894225

INDEX

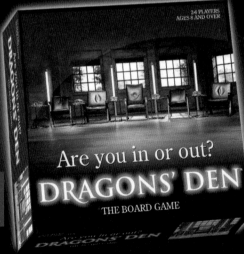